The Secret Carp

Also published by Merlin Unwin Books

The Pursuit of Wild Trout
Mike Weaver
ISBN 1 873674 00 7 £16.95

Trout & Salmon Rivers of Ireland
an angler's guide
Peter O'Reilly
ISBN 1 873674 01 5 £16.95

The One That Got Away
or tales of days when fish triumphed over anglers
Brian Clarke, David Profumo, Max Hastings, David Steel, et al
ISBN 1 873674 02 3 £16.95

A History of Flyfishing
Conrad Voss Bark
ISBN 1 873674 03 1 £25.00

An Angler for all Seasons
the best of H. T. Sheringham
H. T. Sheringham
ISBN 1 873674 04 X £16.95

The Best of Bernard Venables
the illustrated memoir of an angler
Bernard Venables
ISBN 1 873674 06 6 £19.95 (publication April 1993)

The Secret Carp

CHRIS YATES

Chapter opening illustrations by Clare Yates

Merlin Unwin Books

First published in Great Britain by Merlin Unwin Books, 1992
ISBN 1 873674 05 8

Text copyright © Chris Yates, 1992
Illustrations copyright © Clare Yates, 1992

Published by:
Merlin Unwin Books
21 Corve Street
Ludlow
Shropshire SY8 1DA

Distributed by:
Chris Lloyd Sales and Marketing Services
463 Ashley Road
Parkstone, Poole
Dorset BH14 0AX

British Library Cataloguing-in-Publication Data:
A catalogue record for this book is available from the British Library

Designed and typeset in 12 point Goudy by Karen McCall and Tina Mulliner
Printed in Great Britain by Cambridge University Press

Contents

CHAPTER ONE

The Perfect Pool

Any fisherman who dreams of the perfect pool is always hoping that his imagined paradise really exists and that one day he might actually find it. Many years ago I thought I had stumbled on such a place, but because it was night time and a mist was rising I could not, at first, be sure. It was the scent that originally led me to it, the soft, ripe smell of vintage water that is familiar to anyone who has spent half his life fishing for carp by the side of old lakes and ponds. I was on my motorcycle, riding back from a long day's chub stalking on the Sussex Rother, near Petworth. It was late, but instead of making straight for home I took a foolish plunge into a maze of twisting lanes, looking for a particularly fine-sounding pub a friend had told me about. I didn't find it, in fact I got hopelessly lost.

Then the lane I was following dropped into a wooded valley and I found myself passing through a cloud of that sweet evocative scent. It was so strong and so infused with all the other summer smells I associate with carp fishing that I

1

had to stop and investigate. Slowing down meant the scents stopped rushing into my face, but though less concentrated in the stillness, they were just as infectious; a lovely pot-pourri of elder, dog rose, honeysuckle and wild garlic weaving through the denser smell of ancient water like wood smoke weaving through a barn of apples. Somewhere nearby was a pond or a lake and it was essential that I find it. The setting fulfilled all my requirements for perfect carp country: deep valleys, old woods, no obvious signs of habitation and lanes that had more traffic going across than along them (since leaving the main road I'd not seen a single car coming or going, but there had been roe deer, fox, rabbits and a hare crossing in front of me).

Taking off my crash helmet I leant my bike against a fence post and stood in the road listening. I hoped there might be the distant sound of water trickling or rushing over an outfall, but apart from the ticking of the cooling engine, all was silent. The canopy of beech trees reached overhead but there was not, at least, complete darkness. The moon was up, only a few days from full, dappling the lane with vague spots of light. I began walking, looking for an opening through the trees where I might get a better view of my surroundings. After a short distance the tall smooth trunks on my left became stark silhouettes against a weirdly luminous background.

Low-lying roads back along the way had taken me through several pockets of mist and, with the clear night rapidly cooling after a hot day, conditions were pointing towards a fine, fat fog. There seemed to be a hollow lower down the valley, a perfect cup for the kind of mist that wells up from deep tepid stillwater. By dawn it would probably have overflowed and drowned the whole county.

The Perfect Pool

I stepped under the trees towards the light but bramble and blackthorn made an almost impenetrable barrier and I could not find a clear way through. However, after a few jacket-ripping yards I did find a large half-decayed tree stump which improved my view once I had climbed up onto it. Straight away I saw what I had hoped to see.

Between two beech trunks I looked down at what appeared to be an expansive, pear-shaped lake. It was surrounded on three sides by woods, but I could not see anything of the banks because of the mist. The low, early-summer moon was directly overhead and the mist looked as white and as smooth-surfaced as a field of snow. Only by staring at it for several minutes could I detect the slow shifting, the almost imperceptible rising and falling of the upper layers. Then a curious current of air drew a long column of vapour out of the main mass and it rose up, pale and transparent against the trees beyond before detaching itself from its base, only to dissolve and vanish.

Of course, all the while I was thinking that this might be my perfect carp pond. I even hoped I might sniff out the very smell of carp amongst the other scents, for the fish do exude a faint yet distinctive aroma. It does not actually have anything fishy about it, reminding me more of dried herbs and marmalade. There may have been something like that in the air, but it was not strong enough to convince and anyway, carp or no carp, I knew I would have to return in daylight. The place needed exploring properly and I wanted to discover what creatures, if any, haunted it.

I turned to go and as I began wading back through the brambles I heard, in spite of my commotion, a sudden, sharp sound. I froze and listened and it came again: the echoing crash of a heavy fish leaping.

Stupendous carp lived in that lake. It had never been fished, in fact its existence had become almost entirely forgotten by the locals and the owners of the huge estate on which it lay. It was overgrown and inaccessible, its banks a tangled wilderness, its margins speared by reeds, jungled with weeds, bristling with the gnarled branches of drowned, fallen trees. The great fish would emerge from the depths and cruise between and beneath these reefs of dead wood or they would materialise out in the lake's centre, drifting just below the surface, looking like the shadows of passing clouds.

These were the images I carried home with me that night and which grew even more wonderful and improbable in the days that followed, despite the fact that I could not find the lake on my map. Perhaps, I thought, it had been further north than I remembered or maybe, as sometimes happens, the cartographer had, for some reason, failed to show it. However, as a lifelong carpologist and hunter of lakes, I felt my optimism was justified. As well as having the right smell, the place had had the right *feel*.

Since quite early in my angling career, I have had this picture in my head of an ideal carp pool. Moreover, I did not merely hope that such a place existed, I was convinced, even though my vision of perfection, as described above, was rather unusual. All the ingredients though - the unkempt banks, the solitude, the tangled margins, the shadowy depths - all were necessary for that essential and yet indefinable quality: mystery. Every water, from winding brook to mountain tarn, has an element of mystery, but the mystery, the enigma of a carp lake

4

should be deep and profound, as befits the nature of the fish itself. The problem nowadays of course is that, because of over-intensive angling, too many carp waters have had their mystery literally fished out of them. There is Redmire Pool, for

instance, in Herefordshire, a legendary place and once the most magical stillwater in the country. But its jewel-in-the-crown status has now robbed it of much of its enchantment. Over the last forty years it has generated so much interest and attention - much of it of the wrong kind - that its finest quality has become diminished.

But it is not simply a lack of mystery which, to me, can undermine the complete enjoyment of carp fishing. There are many other reasons, some obvious, some obscure, why a lovely looking place could never be called perfect. And, unfortunately, there have also been near-perfect pools that were despoilt and some that have always been denied me.

Beechmore in Devon, deep and dark, encircled by towering trees, seemed the epitome of my ideal but, like

Redmire, it was rather too high up in the carp fishing hierarchy, rather too well-known. Furthermore, I felt that the atmosphere was cool and occasionally even disturbing, as if the pool was a perpetually staring, hostile eye. A much more affable water was Sheepwash, a pool of about three acres set in gently rolling Sussex farmland. When I first visited it, in 1973, it was unknown, undisturbed, unfished. There were plenty of carp, one or two of them very large, there were willows in the water, lilies and vast weed beds. Yet, though it was pretty and despite the fact that I and a few good friends had many enjoyable days there, Sheepwash could sometimes seem prosaic, even bland; it was like a person whose talents you could admire, but whose lack of depth discouraged any lasting friendship.

Abbotsmere, in a green, fertile valley in the Black Mountains, seemed almost perfect when I first fished it, in 1970. It lay in the grounds of a former monastery and had a lovely hallowed air about it; a small pool, not more than two acres, surrounded by crack willows, alders and oaks. The carp were genuine wildies whose ancestry obviously dated back to the time of the monks. Beautiful fish: graceful, streamlined, richly-coloured in various shades of gold, ochre and blue.

In 1972 the pool was unofficially stocked with mirror carp which grew quite large and it was subsequently invaded by anglers for whom size counted for everything. Nothing else mattered in their headlong rush to accumulate carp poundage. The tranquil paradise became littered with beer cans and bait tins; it became crowded; it became depressing. I crossed it off my list.

Another love affair that ended badly concerned Furnace Lake, near Felbridge, Sussex. It was a large, square sheet of water, surrounded by high woods and great beds of reeds. When I first saw it in 1968, I was immediately struck by its quiet grandeur, its cathedral atmosphere. The carp were mostly small wildies, but there were also monsters known through legend and by the occasional tremendous splash as something rose from the depths. I actually hooked one of these mythical creatures on a piece of crust and its inevitable departure still haunts me. For a few years this lake was overflowing the pages of my fishing diary, but then, tragically, a mysterious disease wiped out almost the entire stock. The spirit went out of the place and though it was later restocked (with mirrors) it was never the same again.

There was a chain of carp pools in woodland to the north-east of Lewes, the largest of which, with its overhung bays, its overgrown banks, its wooded island and its clear depths, struck me as one of the most attractive, seductive carp waters I had ever seen. Alas, the owner refused me permission to fish. I discovered another marvellous pond in a dense hazel wood near the village of Dunsfold in Surrey. Reedy, weedy, it was mostly quite shallow and had, despite its tranquillity and remoteness, a uniquely cheerful, optimistic character.

It was also the domain of a colony of immense carp and I thought that even if I never obtained a permit I would still have to fish there, regardless. Then, by chance, I discovered the identity of the owner and my pleading letter was sympathetically replied to. I was given permission to fish there whenever I liked. Yet there are places on earth that are more than simply mysterious. No matter how glorious or magical (or maybe because of their magic) they are somehow impossible to revisit. I still have the owner's letter, dated May 1969, but it's probably too late now to take advantage of it. For all kinds of not very good reasons, I never went back to Dunsfold.

However, ten years later, the mist-shrouded lake preyed more effectively on my imagination and after a few days I knew I had to return. Even in daylight, I presumed it was going to be difficult to find again without a map reference. But, after an hour, chugging aimlessly through the labyrinth of hedged-in, tree-hung lanes, I recognised a landmark, picked up my trail and so came once more to the place where the road had taken a dive into watery incense.

In the breezy afternoon the fragrances were unnoticeable and the air was merely fresh and sweet. Leaning my bike against the same fencepost as before (off the road the turf was too soft for the propstand), I quickly found a straight-forward route through the belt of beeches, avoiding all the thorns and brambles; yet before I reached the edge the trees I suddenly knew exactly what I was going to find. I walked out into an open field and looked down into a wide hollow that bristled with reed tussocks and clumps of sallow, but which contained not even a puddle of water. The mist had been shrouding nothing more than a shrunken marsh.

What I had smelt and seen, however, was a ghost lake for I later discovered that an old lake had, indeed, once stretched across that valley. And the sound of the leaping fish? That might also have been a ghost, but it was more probably the sound of a startled fox or badger turning suddenly in dry leaves. All echo and illusion, brought on by the intoxicating air and a mind too inclined towards carp fishing.

Years passed and I almost gave up my belief in the perfect pool. But now, after a quarter of a century, I think I might have found it ...

CHAPTER TWO

The Angler's Dream

It is 3a.m. on Midsummer morning. I am sitting by a lake. A real lake. What I mean to say is that this is happening now. Writing with letters larger than usual I can just see these words appearing on the page, but the first touch of day is so feeble that the pen-lines melt like smoke if I stare too hard. It is almost two hours before sunrise, and with the world's edge veiled in a fine mist, the lake has become oceanic. Its immense surface, unbroken by ripple, mirrors the faint light and seems to spread beyond the far horizon. If an Atlantic liner steamed through the middle distance or an albatross winged gracefully overhead I think I'd be only mildly surprised.

The air is utterly still and a pallid vapour hangs motionless over the water. For eight or nine hours this stillness has been building like a wall around me, yet the lake has never once been absolutely flat calm. The pale moon looks static in the west, but its reflection slowly spins and sways like a wobbled plate. There is a constant, subtle shifting, like a gentle sea

9

swell, a just-perceptible undulation. Unlike a small pond or pool, which remains completely still on a windless dawn, a large deep lake like this is continually pulsing and stirring with hidden currents and gradually subsiding turbulence - the echoes of yesterday waves. And, of course, there is something else moving down there, unseen as yet, unknown. In fact at the moment it seems unreal, just another fantasy but a powerfully compelling one. Anything that can keep an ordinary mortal from his bed for an entire night must be fairly remarkable. Yet I am no ordinary mortal, I am a dormouse, and I love my bed so much that I have rediscovered the art of hibernation.

Even so, this fantasy has kept me from my pillows more than just once; over the years it has led me through a thousand nights and into almost as many sunrises. It is more fundamental than my dream of the perfect pool, in fact it is the inspiration for that and a score of other such dreams. I call it a 'fantasy' because it seems not only unreal at this moment, but also a little irrational in this day and age. Yet if all goes well, fantasy and reality will eventually converge at a point thirty yards from where I'm now sitting. My line will run out, my rod will curve and, after a suitably dramatic interval, the subject of my fantasy, the inspirer of dreams and fomenter of troubles will come rolling over the net in the shape of a fabulous carp.

For the present though, this lake and its surroundings have been locked under a spell and not even the approaching morning is having an effect on it. Everything has been transfixed by the night: there are no movements, no sounds, nothing to disturb the scene. The woods hang like static grey clouds along the water's edge, the thin mist furls across the distance like cauldron steam, my line droops from the rod like a stitch of old spider's web. The surface tension flexes gently and not even a rising bubble breaks it. Yet the thought that it might break theatrically at any second puts everything into another dimension; my line might cut suddenly across it or perhaps an amazing golden-scaled creature might burst through it. Pure conjecture, I know, and all a consequence of that wretched fantasy; my angler's dream. Yet it sustains me, it will keep me here all day, it charges the atmosphere with marvellous potential, and though there will be times when it loses force and even goes stale, I keep coming back to that happy notion that sooner or later, it will come true, just as my dream of the perfect lake came true.

CHAPTER THREE

A Lord of the Lake

It was like a different world here yesterday. I arrived in the late afternoon and a strong summer wind was blowing down the length of the lake making it look like a swollen fast-running river. The ripples slapped heavily into the dam and these woods, so calm and quiet at the present moment, sounded like a raging sea. I walked halfway round the lake, pausing in gaps between the trees, looking for carp, trying to decide where I was going to fish for the night.

No one else was here and there were no signs that anyone had ever cast from the banks. I know, from the local legends, that big carp haunt this place, but what I find so exciting and fascinating is the fact that, throughout the long history of this lake, no carp angler has ever fished here before - or at least, not until this summer.

Of course it was difficult to see anything below the waves, but I made out a few vague, carp-shaped shadows moving quite swiftly in different directions as they often do in windy conditions, like sailing ships on important voyages. None of them seemed particularly large, however; perhaps the biggest was twelve to fifteen pounds and the rest averaged about eight pounds. I crossed the dam and entered the noisy wood. Then, as I peered into a kind of bay between fallen and leaning trees, I came to a pocket of marvellous silence, as if a glass box had been dropped over my head. The wind still blew and the leaves still hissed but I experienced that same isolating quiet that, say, a gambler in a crowded casino would know if he was suddenly dealt five aces.

The fallen tree on my right protected the area of water in front of me from the worst effects of the wind and the surface just swayed and rocked. In midwater, not twenty feet from the bank and facing away from me, hung the dark mass of an immense carp.

Its tail was outspread, but barely moving and the big pectorals did no more than keep the fish balanced and absolutely motionless. Sunlight, refracted through the shifting surface, ran in flickering bands along its great back and, though I couldn't see every detail, the dark mesh of the scales and the long furling sail of the dorsal were clearly visible. Being so wide across the shoulders I thought it might be a forty pounder, but then it began to swing slowly round until it was broadside on and I saw that, despite its three-foot length, it was not terribly deep and therefore probably weighed in the middle thirties. A superb-looking fish though; dark and compact, it had a kind of solemn majesty that befitted a lord of the lake.

It gave a slight flinch and I guessed that it could feel, if not see, my intensely gazing eyes. If ever a big carp comes closely into my line of sight I always try to look away. After all, the carp, with its acute vision, is almost certainly going to realise that an angler's eager and horrid face has been superimposed over a familiar background; therefore it's best to dissolve into that background by slowly turning your head, then easing back from the water, trying to look indifferent, like a cow or a horse. The trick in carp-watching is to pretend not to watch, but on this occasion I was too fascinated to look away and the fish, intimidated by my constant stare, began to de-materialise. It sank lower and then, with a single flick of the tail, curved away and melted into the depths.

I didn't need to look any further and decided straight away to pitch in near to that place. Not right in it, though. It would be tricky enough to fish in broad daylight, but the menacing jungle of twisting, submerged boughs would have made it suicidal at night. So I chose a spot by a lily bed, where there was a convenient gap in the trees, about twenty five yards down the bank. From there I could cast just to the edge of the first sunken branch and hope that, if the carp returned and I hooked it, I could steer it into the open water in front of me. I scattered sweetcorn - a bait the fish had probably never seen before - round the area, then went and fetched the rest of my gear from my van, parked nearby.

By the time I had tackled up my rod (a lissom split cane creation called the *Bishop*), prepared my net and made a cup of tea, the wind had begun to lessen. And by the time I was in position, with the bait cast to the chosen spot and my few bits and pieces ready to hand, the waves were beginning to smooth away into a gentle swell and the trees around me were easing towards stillness.

Then across the lake the sun went down and for a while everything glowed like a smouldering tangerine.

Fluttering bats appeared, cutting across the curving flight paths of swallows and swifts; the first big, slow moths hovered over the bankside vegetation, looking for nectar. Gradually, the warm glow shrank into the north-west, leaving the world layered with blues and greens and in the distance a carp pencilled a pale line on the surface.

Soon the birds had finished their evening chorus and the swallows and swifts left the airways for the bats. Before it became properly dark I reeled in, rebaited and cast again. Though I couldn't see the exact position of the nearest submerged tree I tried not to be too timid and aimed to get the bait as near the carp's sanctuary as possible. Naturally I overdid it and got hooked up. But as I pulled for a break the line suddenly sprang free and everything seemed all right when I checked it. I cast again, less recklessly, but was faintly troubled by thoughts of chafed line and strained hooks. A more cautious angler would have tied on a new trace (I was using a yard of 12lb b.s. braided nylon) and a new hook.

The afterglow shifted perceptibly round to the north and was visible until midnight when the strengthening moonlight obscured it. Four or five days after full, the moon must have risen at around eleven o'clock, but I had no sight of it until much later. It was low to the south and the trees round the lake were only dimly illuminated. By midnight the occasional distant road-drone and the faint eddyings of breeze had all ceased; apart from the whisper of water going over the outfall, there was perfect silence.

Never perfect calm, though. The image of that great carp, banded with sunlight, was still vivid in my mind; in fact it grew brighter as darkness fell. Under the black lake it had probably returned to its haunt and would almost certainly come across the scattering of corn. I could imagine its huge, shadowy form, now flickering with moonlight, as it sniffed, cat-like round

the bait. At any moment the foil on the line might jump and rustle and signal a take, and though I leaned back comfortably against my creel and tried to concentrate on counting meteors, I was never completely relaxed. I've only fished here a couple of times before and this was my first complete night and day - a full twenty four hours. Though the fish had no reason to be nocturnal, I felt it was more likely to feed confidently at night.

The hours wore on and the sense of imminent drama gradually gave way to weariness. The words of a nonsense rhyme kept going round in my head 'Up above the sky so high, like a tea-tray in the sky.' There were no splashes across the lake, no sudden swirls on the dark surface, no signs that even a small carp inhabited the place. There was only the thin squeaking of young moorhens, a sharp cry of some other unidentified bird, the owls, the soft flutter of the bats. I didn't sleep. I didn't even doze. It was my first night at a perfect lake and I didn't want to miss anything. I wanted to savour every moment of it, even the moments of tedium and discomfort.

Several times I heard rustling footsteps moving through the wood behind me and once something approached and paused. I could feel it watching me. It shambled un-hurriedly and invisibly away and I'm sure it was a badger. There were certainly deer, fox and rabbit as well and also the inevitable little scurryings and scratchings of mice, voles and shrews. But there were no human sounds round this great expanse of water, no other angler waited for the dawn. The lake and the night were solely for the animals, the moths, the glow-worms, the carp and me.

Nights can have all kinds of different qualities: they can be tense and brittle or heavy and oppressive, they can be cold, bland and boring: this one was serene and luminous. There was no total darkness, even in my pitch under the eaves of the wood, and at around 3 a.m. a grey forelight began to take the shine out of the moon. Mist began to form across the lake and for the first time a shiver of cold went through my bones. Then I noticed a waiter with a loaded tea trolley slowly advancing toward me. I blinked, the waiter vanished and to my great delight I remembered that my dear Gaffer had thoughtfully packed me a hot flask. I'd said that, as I was bringing my stove, I wouldn't need it, but she knew I could never bring myself to make tea in the middle of the night and so slipped a life-saver into a tackle bag. I sneaked back to the van to fetch it and it was still hot. Within five minutes I'd drunk the entire contents, restoring my body temperature, my optimism, my faith in carp fishing, my appreciation of the night and my sanity.

CHAPTER FOUR

Dawn

It is now, as I write, about an hour before sunrise and the grey world is being invaded by colour. The leaves and reeds are turning green, and the yellow is seeping gloriously into the iris in front of me. All night these things were merely black silhouettes and to watch them coming to life is like seeing their true colours for the first time. No sounds yet, apart from the odd call of the waterfowl. (Did I imagine a distant skylark just then?) And no movements, apart from that slow hypnotic stirring on the surface and the indefinable shifting of the mist. I reeled in a few minutes ago and the bait was untouched. Perhaps the big carp was only passing by yesterday. Perhaps the drowned forest is not his permanent sanctuary. But still I have that feeling that he may come back.

What's this? A disturbance! The first real intrusion into the scene for hours. Some creature is approaching along the margins. It turns out to be nothing more amazing than a young coot, staggering across the lily bed to my right with all the grace and poise of a drunkard dancing on a dinner table. It teeters between two pads, lurches forward and flumps down with a splosh. Now it is in open water, chugging straight past me, oblivious of my presence. A thrush drops a couple of notes into the silence, testing its depth. Blackbird next, just a brief phrase, now a cuckoo, echoing, very far off. Blackbird and thrush singing a duet. Now a woodpigeon, his voice seeming to have no source or penetration, yet it fills the dawn with sound.

My line moved then. Where it slants into the water there is a little blister in the surface tension and, out of the corner of my eye, I saw this blister tremble. Because I'm now staring directly at it, it'll probably not move again, but the air still crackles with tension. Out in the lake are no signs that a fish might be feeding, no bubbles or mud clouds to reveal the presence of a truffling carp. Again! Again the line signals some secret life. It swings up into a more pronounced diagonal, but falls loosely back again. Maybe a small fish is toying with the bait. I have three grains of corn on a size eight (weighted with a three swan-shot link) and perhaps ...

Just then came a wonderful disruption. The line tightened and remained taut and I was convinced a fish had picked up the bait and was simply hovering in mid-water with it, ruminating over it. Suddenly it cut even tighter through the surface and I dropped everything, snatched up the rod and struck. But there was no contact. Nothing at all. Perhaps it was, as I said, only a tiddler. You can never be sure. I rebait and recast. I compose myself once again, brush the dry mud off this page and recover my pen from a clump of watermint.

Frankly, the idea of a thunderous great carp smashing up the dawn is not quite as appealing as it should be, considering I'm meant to be an incurable carper. I was not,

22

however, quite prepared. It would have been a major upheaval after the night's tranquillity. I'm not just consoling myself for my failure: four o'clock in the morning is too early to wrestle with Leviathan. It's interesting, though, that I feel like this. Had it

been twenty years ago I would not now be sitting back, scribbling and being objective, I would have been poised over the rod waiting for another twitch of the line.

Obviously time mellows passion, but it might also have something to do with the fact that ten years ago my fishing dream, my ideal image, underwent a metamorphosis, changing from a carp in a dark pool to a barbel in a fast, clear river. It had happened before. Once it changed into a chub and then into a tench, but it had always returned to its original carp form and so I presumed I would remain addicted for the rest of my life. But then, in 1982, I discovered barbel and actually believed that the old affliction had been permanently cured, that my new love for rapid, transparent streams would save me from silting up beside ancient, monster-haunted ponds.

For almost ten years I was an obsessive barbel angler. I even moved house to get closer to my favourite river. Of course there was the occasional dalliance with my old flame, but that was just out of nostalgia. Now I have found this lake and suddenly the barbel has sunk lower in the water and the carp has risen up again and become incandescent. Yet, because I find barbel and their rivers so compelling they won't fade completely from sight and so I shall probably be spared another bout of total carpophilia. I can even be blasé about missed strikes.

I had hoped to note down each new voice as it joined the dawn chorus, but already - perhaps only twenty minutes since that thrush first broke the silence, just before my line moved - the entire avian male voice choir has reached crescendo pitch. The wood behind me is ringing like a bell and there are scores of songsters, most of whom I recognise and some that I don't, all shouting their heads off. Across the lake the waterfowl, with their harsher calls, are the percussion section of this orchestra: quacking, shrieking, clicking, rasping and croaking. Another day has begun.

CHAPTER FIVE

Discovery and Exploration

As I am facing west it seems, at the moment, as if the tree line opposite is about to ignite. The fog-rinsed colours are almost pulsing with light and yet the sun has still not quite risen. A heron descends through the mist, turns and - Woosh! I think I rattled him. He obviously wanted to perch on the half-sunken branch right here in the margins, but just as he was putting on the air brakes, he spotted me, wheeled round and flapped off up the lake. Now a band of sunlight has touched the upper edge of the tree line. Even as I watch the luminous green is turning gold and this glow is extending lower and lower down the trees, until within ten minutes, the entire skyline is ablaze.

Here, where I am fishing in the shadow of the wood on the eastern bank, I won't be able to see or feel the sun directly for at least five hours and my cave-like viewpoint makes the far-off, mist-filtered illuminations seem unearthly. Time passes and the distances become even more illusory as the strengthening sun gives substance to the mist.

This is the first dawn I've ever seen here and I shan't forget it. Yet it seems very odd that until a fortnight ago, I had never even set eyes on this place. I had heard about it several years ago, after my angling companion Bob James first stumbled on it. He described it glowingly and after enquiries, discovered that it was inhabited by perch, trout and some impressive common carp. But he also discovered that there was no possibility of fishing it. The lake is set in ancient and very exclusive parkland, patrolled by keepers and fishing was, then, absolutely forbidden. Had this been in my pre-barbel fishing days, when I was still obsessed by carp, I would certainly have wanted to investigate further, but as it happened I was only mildly curious. I still had too many rivers to explore.

Then, not long ago, a carp connoisseur and local hero told me that, after years of patient negotiations, he'd finally been granted permission to form a small syndicate on the lake. Furthermore, Bob and I were honoured with an invitation to join this group and so I was subsequently privy to a much more complete history of the place, a history rich in probable and improbable stories and fables. Thus the vague mental picture I had of the lake became more vivid and evocative and it was suddenly urgently necessary to see it for myself. It sounded uncannily similar to that dream water I'd given up looking for.

I went down with Bob on the first day of this season, not to fish, but to explore and decide whether we should join the syndicate. Bob, like me, was delighted with the prospect of fishing here, but was not sure that he had the time or the money for a permit. I didn't have the money either, nor do I actually desire as much fishing time as I used to, especially now that I have young children with their own dreams and a whole new world for me to walk them through. However, there was no point in making any decisions until we'd both had a good look round.

We approached the lake from a ruined house on the western side, where great trees towered up from the bank. Because of them, we couldn't see the lake's full extent, but I had the impression of a vast acreage stretching away limitlessly north and south. The water had a curious jade tint, like the colour of the sea round chalk cliffs and it appeared to be immensely deep. It was evening and the surface was calm. The trees cast enormous elongated shadows across the water, but the sun was still strong on the far bank. We turned under the heavy foliage and walked a quarter of a mile down to the dam, crossed it and entered this wood on the east bank.

Immediately we began to see the shapes of carp, basking in the last warmth of the day. There were a dozen at least cruising in that bay where I saw the monster yesterday, but the biggest was not above ten pounds. Where a single ancient oak lay decomposing in the margins something much larger, but deep and shadowy, came slowly into view. It turned and hung in midwater so that I could train my binoculars on it (the binoculars that I foolishly left behind yesterday!). As I looked, three other, even bigger fish ghosted into focus. They were not giants, but they must all have been around twenty pounds. Later, we saw several other big carp, but no monsters. However, even if I'd seen only a few mediocre specimens, I would still have come to the same decision. I *had* to fish there.

It was a magnificent lake, heavy with atmosphere, rich in all those quirky characteristics I had been looking for. It also had the correct specific gravity for a good monster water and looked as if it could produce a hundred pounder before breakfast. Furthermore, there was so much of it and it possessed such a glorious range of qualities, from the sublime to the eccentric. In fact it was like an amalgam of all my favourite old carp waters, with its ancient echoes and its sense of past glories going wonderfully to seed. Along the banks were the broken remains of classical statues festooned with ivy, shrouded with ferns; great trees lay in the margins where they had fallen, bleached and skeletal, like the bones of dinosaurs; bizarre obelisks reared up out of the forest of vegetation; there were crumbling follies, overgrown paths, a bat-haunted grotto, all fragments of an extravagant dream succumbing to reality. Unlike its surroundings, the water itself had an air of perm-anence about it; another millennium might pass and its serene expression would remain unaltered. Compared with the ghastly almost suburban uniformity of many of the country's present carp waters, this was - *is* - paradise.

And of course I would have to fish here anyway, because of the carp. They were an unknown quantity, with no estate records of their introduction; in fact they appeared always to have existed here. There were true old English wildies swimming alongside a more portly type of common, with a high back and a deep belly and there was also a group that was obviously a cross between the two; larger than the wildies but leaner than the commons. The average size of the total pop-ulation seemed not much over ten pounds yet several enormous aristocarp had been seen, including one so huge it was at first presumed to be a big cloud of disturbed mud. The only large carp ever recorded was a 37-pounder shot by a former keeper as it was basking in the shallow bay.

Though Bob was impressed, he wasn't quite as enthusiastic as me and he finally decided against joining the syndicate. However, he may change his mind by next season. So the first time I fished here was last week when I came, alone, on a lovely grey humid evening, just as the light began to sink. It had been raining and the air was laden with the scent of wet

grass and damp woods. From certain trees there came a thin screaming of a million hovering insects but, apart from a shrill thrush, all the birds had fallen silent.

I walked along the bank until I came to a place overhung by alders where a sandy shelf extended beneath the surface, twenty yards out. During a previous reconnaissance I'd seen several large carp making clear silhouettes of themselves as they drifted back and forth across this shelf and I thought it seemed a good place for my first cast.

I crept under the trees, scattered a pound of sweetcorn just beyond the margins and cast my baited hook into the midst of it. I rested the rod in a forked stick (I do have a proper rod rest, but I'd forgotten it), put a fold of silver foil over the line above the reel, sat back on an old coat and let my inactivity heal the hole I'd made in the stillness.

The carp were, of course, uneducated in the ways of anglers, but I have found that such ignorance never makes them easier to catch. Their natural caution, always highly developed, seems to approach a supernatural awareness at times, and this is always more apparent in a wild or semi-wild environment. With so many carp waters now run as commercial carp fisheries, and the fishes behaviour conditioned by the activities of anglers, it is easy to forget or dismiss the old stories of the first carp specialists. These pioneers often found that the fish were almost unapproachable, let alone uncatchable, and an entire season could pass without a single bite.

Carp are quick to learn, they learn, in fact, faster than any other fish - mainly because they have a larger brain. But the learning still takes time because they will always be more cautious than curious. They will grow accustomed to the shape of an angler on the bank, but only if that shape is a constant presence over a long period; they learn to come to an angler's groundbait, but only if it is presented more or less continually for days and days on end. Of course there are always exceptions to this rule.

If only one solitary angler is fishing a lake for a small colony of carp then it may be weeks or even months before he persuades a fish to take his bait. Conversely, on a hard-banked, well-stocked carp water, where the fish are experienced in the ways of anglers and familiar with every kind of exotic bait, it can take less than ten minutes to find the carp and even less time to catch one. The fish do not fade like smoke at the first, albeit cautious, approach of the fisherman. As long as he makes no abrupt movements or vibrations with his boots they will regard him as no more menacing than a bankside tree. But, in the wild state, a carp can sometimes melt away merely at the angler's presence, no matter how craftily he conceals himself. There will be times, though, when none of these things hold true, for carp can also be the most unpredictable creatures.

On that first night the carp were conforming to type and, apart from a sudden, rustling lift of the foil, there were, initially, no signs and not even any sense of them in my vicinity (I think the abrupt tightening of the line was more to do with a bat flying into it than a fish testing the bait).

However at around midnight, there was a distant yet tremendous splash as some great fish turned on the surface. Though it must have been nearly 200 yards away it sounded hugely impressive in the silence and the noise echoed weirdly in the woods opposite. I stared out across the lake, but it was some time - maybe three minutes - before the dark semi-circle of ripple came spreading towards me.

Perhaps the monster had woken. Perhaps something had got under its scales and now it was on the rampage, its appetite sharpened by the conditions. Especially on such a perfect fishing night - warm, almost tropical after a day of rain - I presumed all the fish would have discovered a great hunger and I was sure they'd feel the need to sup on sweetcorn. I cast again and awaited further messages of hope. But there was nothing more; just the bats, the owlet above my head squeaking like a child's toy, a scuttling mouse, the drip-drip of wet leaves and my simmering expectation. It was enough.

CHAPTER SIX

Present Location

 A single shaft of sunlight has filtered through the foliage behind me and is dappling this page. It might be a good omen. Overhead, half the sky is obscured by the eaves of the wood as it shelves down across the water's edge. There are beech and alder, but the dominant tree here is an ancient and magnificent oak whose great boughs spread wider and reach higher than any other tree at this end of the lake. I am sitting very comfortably on my folded coat, leaning back against my creel and facing north-west, so that I'm looking more up the lake than across it.

Tall grass, nettles, watermint and hogweed crowd round me and one of the greatest delights of this place is in its untrammelled wilderness appearance. Moreover, with the crumbling bits of stonework and overgrown paths, it is like a wilderness making a victorious advance rather than the usual bludgeoned withdrawal.

There are no signs of angling activity and certainly no neatly-levelled pitches with all nearby branches carefully trimmed to allow convenient casting. There are no platforms or other ugly little luxuries so beloved by angling institutions. I realise such things are necessary at a populous lake where bank erosion and general hacking down of greenery would otherwise occur, but I have always disliked any sign of formal organisation when I'm fishing. To be corralled like a sheep on an official, purpose-built fishing platform is demeaning and inhibiting: it cramps the style and destroys the spirit of adventure which, surely, is essential if you are to enjoy angling to the full.

Over the years I have witnessed all kinds of carefully orchestrated vandalism at once-beautiful lakes and ponds. I remember one suburban-minded club, paranoid about such things as reed-beds and overhanging vegetation who scythed round an entire pool with everything from chainsaws to a J.C.B. transforming it from a lovely willow-fringed carp water into a puddled crater in a ploughed field. Thankfully, such desecration will not happen here and there are enough gaps in the trees for the more conventional anglers to fish comfortably without having to resort to saw and axe. The more adventurous types can explore all kinds of secret, almost inaccessible, corners where you have to crawl and creep to reach the water's edge and where there's every chance of coming face-to-face with some unsuspecting monster.

Except for one sunken branch, the margins are clear in front of me and, apart from the lilies, the nearest dangerous snags live in the drowned arboretum 25 yards to my right. Even if I hadn't seen that huge carp yesterday I think I would have probably chosen this spot to fish. The wind has been in the same direction for a week, blowing down the lake, and I think the carp here would be especially prone to being wind-herded. Though there is no movement of air at all at present, all my carp fishing experience shows that even the faintest breeze will eventually move the fish along its direction and they will remain more-or-less downwind until it swings from a different quarter. Hence the popularity of pitches on the east banks of carp lakes; hence my fondness for a strong east wind which will move the carp into areas where they rarely congregate and are therefore less disturbed by the majority of anglers.

There is, however, no absolute guarantee that all the fish will behave thus and on small sheltered pools wind direction is of little consequence; but I have always felt very confident fishing into the face of a strong steady summer wind. Some of my best carp have been caught under those conditions, and yet I must confess that my idea of a perfect day is to fish from dawn to dusk by a totally flat calm carp pond. Complete stillness may not be the best conditions for catching carp, but after many hours of such tranquillity you can sometimes catch a different kind of magic.

Which brings me to another important reason for choosing this spot. I like it. I like the prospect it gives. I like the immediate surroundings and the atmosphere here better than, say, the place where I first fished, last week. A really barbed-nosed carp angler would never admit to choosing a pitch simply because he liked the look of it. In fact a really barbed-nosed carp angler - and there are a lot of them about nowadays - never admits to liking anything. But feeling happy about your chosen pitch obviously ensures you'll fish more confidently than if you'd felt indifferent towards it. More importantly, you are going to enjoy yourself whether or not you catch anything.

Naturally an angler desires to catch a fish, but so much poppycock is written about 'success' and the mindless striving for 'results' that people forget about the more essential quality, enjoyment. It does not really matter where you fish, what tackle you use, what bait you choose or whether you wear a tweed hat or a traffic cone; if you enjoy your fishing, if you can find interest or entertainment or adventure or peace of mind then you have succeeded. Richard Walker once told me that the most successful angler he knew had never caught anything bigger than a half pound roach, in fact he hardly ever caught anything, but he never failed to enjoy his fishing enormously. However, I know I will like this place even better if I can catch a carp from it.

Being at the downwind end of the lake there is also the added bonus of the incense. All kinds of nostril-tingling fragrances are collecting here. There is the slightly acid smell of wet mud and the more pervasive smell of the water itself, like the smell of steam from a cup of tea. There is the sharp tang of crushed watermint and bruised nettles, the fruit sweetness of elderflower, the metallic bitterness of hogweed, the lovely fume of honeysuckle. In fact, whenever I feel hungry, I need only breathe deeply enough and I could probably sustain myself without food for a week.

Though I suspect I'll be stalking along the banks later in the day I intend to remain in this spot for several hours yet. Apart from the afore-mentioned reasons for being here and the thought of that big carp, pitching in quietly for such a long period is the best way to familiarise myself with the unusual character of this lake. I'll never normally stay for more than an hour in any one place when I'm after carp, except when I'm night fishing. In fact it's been years since I last fished like this, so passive, so sedentary.

Once I've got to know a carp water I much prefer to stalk round the banks until I find a feeding or basking fish. I'm too impatient to wait for the carp to find me. Once I've found what I'm looking for it is a simple matter to put the Yates Theory of Angling into practical operation: present a feeding or inquisitive fish with an acceptable bait without arousing its suspicions and you will probably catch it, even if you're using a beanpole stolen from the garden.

If I sit still for long enough, though, I shall melt gradually into the bankside. The heron and the dabchick, the voles and finally the carp will all accept me as part of the surroundings and I shall be able to watch them behaving more naturally. The more I sink into the landscape, the more easily will I adjust to its subtle rhythms and the closer I'll get to that moment when I'll predict the carp's movements without even thinking.

CHAPTER SEVEN

The Vanishing Lake

I know it's six o'clock because I can hear the hour being struck by a church clock over a mile away. The mist has now dispersed, the dawn chorus is over and the sunlight is already quite hard on the treeline opposite. Yet still the surface of the lake remains unbroken. This is very strange. Not even a rising trout when in the past I have seen dozens of the daft creatures leaping simultaneously, like a juggler's knives. A swan cleaved past an hour ago and a fight broke out between a coot and a moorhen, but nothing has broken through from that other world below and my line has not signalled further contact with it. In fact, had I not actually seen the inhabitants of this water I might by now be thinking that all the stories I've heard about them were pure fiction. Yet had this been so, I'd still have found them irresistible.

There is possibly little truth in the stories from Loch Ness but this doesn't stop people becoming intrigued by them. Furthermore, I remember that half the carp waters I fished as a boy might never have contained any carp at all, or even any fish, and yet my fishing could not have been more exciting. The anticipation was nearly always enough and even before I had cast I could imagine the shock of contact with a monster. And though there have been many times since those early days, when the imagined contact became actual, when physical reality confirmed the truth of some unlikely legend, it was the legend and the element of drama surrounding it that gave the fishing its edge and its depth. An old pond rich in historic myth was always worth more than a municipal park lake and a net full of fish. And, besides the better quality of atmosphere at the old haunts, there was always the potential for some staggering discovery, which was rarely the case at the more populous places.

So I have always been a sucker for stories about secret lakes and although other anglers are also prone to glowing eyeballs at the mention of such waters they are usually more rational and ultimately more sceptical than me. Even 'B.B.', one of the most romantic of angling writers, could not at first believe a story which began circulating in 1951, of a secret pool which had just yielded up a 31 pound carp. At that time such a fish was unimaginable, even to 'B.B.'. But he eventually followed up the story and it led him to the banks of Redmire Pool, the most extraordinary carp water in the country.

As some folk collect fossils or old bottles, so I collected legends of secret lakes, and sometimes I collected the lakes themselves. Over the years I followed up stories that were often ridiculous, sometimes comic, always fascinating and which occasionally, like now, led me to a priceless gem. In the beginning I wasn't looking for the perfect water, that search came later.

In my earliest fishing years I simply wanted to track down any secluded pond that had a reputation for carp Being more gullible then, I sometimes believed every word of even the most extravagant rumour, but though experience toned down my expectation it never spoilt my enthusiasm. And it sometimes happened that a newly-discovered water really did harbour some monstrous carp. Exactly twenty years ago as I write, veteran carp angler ...

A kingfisher has just flared up onto the half-submerged branch in front of me. He didn't arrive by using his wings, but simply appeared by magic. Though in shadow, the

colours of his plumage are still brilliant, especially the electric blue of the head and back. If I moved more than this pen he would instantly vanish, but he seems not to mind me even though he did just fix me with a beady stare. He bobs and suddenly drops downwards through the surface with a little untidy splash. Immediately he returns, in a shower of droplets, to his perch, but there is nothing in his beak. Perhaps he is just bathing and not fishing. Now he simply sits and stares across the water.

As I was saying: Twenty years ago veteran carp angler Tom Mintram, who had just caught a 38-pounder from Redmire, told me a wondrous story about a Kentish lake. A Cranbrook schoolboy had written to him, saying that while fishing for tench at an unnamed water he had spotted some fantastically huge carp. Naturally he had tried to fish for them, but had failed completely. (The kingfisher has just flown off). So he'd written, asking for advice and, impressed by certain convincing details in the letter, Tom decided he would have to see the water for himself. However, on the day he met the boy and was guided to the lake, it was cold and windy.

'To be candid,' said Tom (I have my old fishing diary with me and can therefore quote precisely), 'I didn't see anything. But it had the look of a good carp water. It was covered with lilies and there were reeds which spread over two-thirds of it and stretched towards a big old house - you could see the tall fancy chimneys poking up in the distance. The boy made me vow never to tell anyone else about the lake and I was sure no-one else had fished there recently. But this was five years ago and I never saw the lad again.'

Tom had not imagined he would return, but the lake preyed on his mind and within a few weeks it drew him back. However, without the boy to guide him, it took him three weekends to rediscover it (he'd foolishly not marked it down on a map at the time). 'It was a warm August afternoon when I eventually found it again and after I'd had a look around I climbed a big old oak and watched the lilies moving gently below me. Something was swimming about amongst the pads. Then I saw them! If I wanted a record fish and didn't have Redmire I would definitely fish there. The lad was not mistaken. They were big carp all right.'

I didn't 'have' Redmire at the time, but though I did not have any real ambition to catch a record carp either, Tom's story, so packed with the stuff of legend, naturally caused me to burst into flames. As he said, it was five years since he'd seen the lake, he still had no map references and could only vaguely recall its location. He scratched down rough directions and, soon afterwards, with my brother Nick riding pillion as navigator, I set off into deepest Kent.

Of course we took an O.S. map with us, but Tom's directions did not seem to bear much relationship with it; we homed in on various blue dots in the area Tom had indicated and explored a number of quite exquisite lakes and ponds, but not one of them matched the original description. We did, though, discover a splendid old pub near Goudhurst, and while we were washing down the dust of our journey we mentioned its purpose to the landlord and stirred in him firstly a dim memory and then a clearer recollection. We showed him Tom's rough map and he decided that a couple of important details had been left out (deliberately? we wondered). We therefore re-drew the map and continued our search, encouraged by the landlord's guidance, inspired by his ale.

The day was fading into a still, warm evening. It was mid July, the soft fruit harvest had been better than anyone could remember and every farm we rode past smelt like a pot of strawberry jam. As the first stars emerged we finally arrived at the 'X' on our revised map: The Mill Pond, Sandway. It was reedy, there were large fish moving near the surface. There was an old house beyond the reed beds on the far bank.

But it was not Tom's secret carp lake. We thought for a while that it might be, but I made a quick sketch in the twilight and when we showed it to Tom the next day he had to disappoint us, though even he said it was a close approximation. The Mill Pond, however, had had no lilies and there were no big trees overhanging the water. Moreover, Tom was convinced that his lake was nowhere near Sandway.

We searched once more, drew a blank, and so couldn't help the growing suspicion that Tom was only remembering a tantalising dream. But during the third quest there were suddenly more allelujias than when Columbus discovered America. Following a long sloping track down into a wooded valley we saw, as our new map reader, G. Jasper Tucker, said we should see, a flash of water between ancient trees. And there it was, precisely as Tom had described, perfectly fitting the frame our imaginations had prepared for it. A densely overgrown lake, the water retreating before an invasion of reeds, the only open stretch limited to a narrow strip along the tree-hung dam. Even here, yellow water lilies clustered thickly along the margins. All around us were the remains of an ancient park drowning under a wild profusion of willow, hazel and oak scrub (far more of a tangled wilderness than this place). The roof and ornate chimneys of a seventeenth century mansion were visible in the distance but we guessed it had been abandoned long ago.

There were no traces of angling activity, no signs of any recent disturbance and certainly no signs that read 'carp fishing prohibited'. (Twenty years ago it was still possible to discover a neglected lake and fish it without seeking permission and without fear of any seriously depressing consequences should we be discovered by a keeper or landowner. If this did happen, which was rare, the innocent, diplomatic and mildly ingratiating manner usually did the trick, with the result that permission to fish was usually given, free of charge. Happy days!).

Without doubt, the lake smelt of carp, but though there were mysterious movements in the lily beds, we didn't actually see anything clearly. It was a cool, grey afternoon and the fish were probably low in the water. We were not, anyway, particularly concerned about the carp on that first visit. It was enough of an achievement just to have found the secret lake.

The weather was much improved on the next trip, when for the first time in years, a bait was cast among the lilies. Unfortunately only Nick and Jasper savoured that moment and I was somehow prevented from being there. I cannot recall now exactly why, but it must have been something fairly earth-shattering, like an engine seizure or perhaps an invitation to tea with Faye Dunaway. Anyway, apart from a few tench and roach, neither angler connected with anything remarkable, though once again they observed stirrings and ripplings in the lilies as something substantial pushed through them. With more time and more bait going in, perhaps we would tempt one of those monsters.

Another trip was arranged, but we never had another cast because, during our absence, a freak thunderstorm had caused the water level to rise so abruptly and so high that the ancient clay dam had suddenly burst and the entire lake, with all the carp and tench and everything else, had simply vanished into the wooded valley below. When we returned there was nothing left except an area of crazed, sun-baked mud and a gently rippling sea of reeds.

CHAPTER EIGHT

The Art of Tea-making

Another undisturbed hour slips by and I have reached three inescapable conclusions. It is said that too much absorption in dream, myth and fable points to a dangerous void in the mind and to save ourselves from deception and disillusion we should stick to the clear paths of logic, fact and truth. But only a half-wit could regard this as wisdom. Logic can take you just one step down any dark road; the only fact that prevails in this world is that there are no certainties; the greatest truth is that you cannot make a good cup of tea with a tea bag.

I had suddenly realised my need for another cup of tea, so I collected a few twigs and put the kettle on. But instead of bothering to walk back the short distance to the van for a packet of best Ceylon I just dipped into my creel and found a tea bag jumbled up with the usual flotsam. The first sip of the resulting cup was dire enough to spit over my boots.

Now I have just reboiled the Kelly Kettle (the greatest steam engine since Stephenson's Rocket) and, using

47

proper tea and a proper tea pot, I am sitting back with a delectable cup of Britain's favourite beverage. A small plume of steam rises into the cool, early-morning air and, apart from a twinge of regret, I savour a moment of bliss. My regret is that, because the majority of the country drink bag tea, they are missing out on the superior cup that only the loose leaves can provide. No wonder the country is going to the dogs. I admit that my bag was not the freshest but even ...

How many times has that happened? A psychologist, a physicist and a freshwater biologist should join forces to discover why a fish so often takes the bait just at the moment when the angler is sipping his tea. I must have been holding my cup in my left hand when, for the first time in ten hours, the foil indicator lifted to the rod. Tea and pen went in opposite directions and my strike put a superb hooping bend in the rod. And that was it. The moment I had been waiting for, the incomparable moment of contact when the world disappears, time stands still and I wonder how many knots I have in my line.

Nothing much happened to begin with except that the pressure on the rod pulsed as if the fish were hitting the lake bed with a mallet. The tip bounced and rebounded, then lurched suddenly into a deep low curve and the reel began to sing. Naturally the image of the big fish came vividly to mind and I leaned everything to the left, trying to coerce whatever it was away from the snags and into open water.

It was obviously a carp and obviously a good one. Much to my surprise it set off in the desired direction, towards the horizon. For a while I was happy to let him travel without much luggage, pleased to see him sailing further and further away from the reefs. But, of course, the greater his distance from me the more potential there was for disaster and I suddenly realised, after about 30 yards of line had gone, that my fish would only have to turn to port and put on full power and I'd be scuppered. With his momentum and my pressure he could actually sweep in beyond the underwater jungle, snagging or snapping the line easily.

So I came down firmly on the reel and, initially, only effected the bend of the cane; the carp chugged on, un-impressed and I became convinced that it was his lordship. The line stretched to within an ounce of its breaking strain, but then

the fish's movements grew more laboured and I felt it rising in the water. I was more confident then. To raise a big fish from deep water and keep it near the surface is often a sign that it'll soon be on the bank. The carp rose almost to the top then rolled and dived, causing a silvery wreath of a swirl which gradually unfurled across the entire corner of the lake. He went round in a couple of slow, deep circles, then, just as I began gaining some line, he swung off in absolutely the wrong direction. Though I hauled, wound and shouted, he homed directly back on the place where he'd picked up the bait and I was powerless to stop him.

There is a kind of ledge about fifteen yards out where the lake bed slopes steeply away. As my fish came up over this ledge towards the sunken trees, so a smooth, bulging wave appeared, travelling fast. Just before disaster struck I eased right off and was amazed to see the carp roll on the surface, as if knocked off balance. It didn't look nearly as big as I'd expected. Though I failed to get a truly clear view, it was obviously no monster, though it may have been a twenty-pounder.

I piled on the sidestrain again, reminding the fish of its unfinished business. It plunged and wound me directly round dead, unyielding wood. There was another bumping swirl, then a terrible grinding heave and the world and I parted company.

A bow wave surged back into open water, petering out where the lake suddenly deepened. My carp sank out of the morning's reality and became a dream again.

CHAPTER NINE

From the List of the Lost

Another cup of tea. My hand still trembles. It is ridiculous, even pathetic, considered objectively. I have only lost a fish, yet I feel as if something vitally important has been stolen from me, some tremendous revelation denied me. I can remember Dick Walker writing somewhere that no-one could possibly imagine the feelings experienced by an angler who has just lost a much-dreamed-about fish. Describing his abrupt separation from a near-record tench, Walker wrote 'I have never been more bitterly disappointed since I first began fishing; it was like finding one's house has been burnt down or one's bank balance (if any) has been embezzled.' I was still a boy when I first read that passage and it delighted me to learn that my hero suffered the same kind of griefs as me.

I had, even then, plenty of experience of that desolate emotional state that follows the loss of some splendid specimen, though in my case it wasn't like having my house burnt down or my money embezzled, it was more like having all my Dinky toys run over by a steam roller. No, it was worse even than that. And I think the sense of loss is deeper and keener when you are young because you are convinced there will never again be such a momentous opportunity. There is certainly no room in your head for any philosophical resignation.

But though the frustration was deeper when I was a sapling, it still grates when it happens now. Here I am, thirty years an angler, I've caught the biggest carp in Britain, and my heart still sinks in the downswirl of another lost fish. There is, in fact, a lake in my head exclusively haunted by dozens of marvellous, tantalisingly-glimpsed carp, fish that never quite were, but always shall be, forever more. And though the successful landing of a few grand patriarchs has consoled me for the loss of others, it is curious how the ones that got away remain more vivid in my mind than the ones that didn't.

Everything is now as it was. The rod is back on its rest, the tackle having been re-tied and the bait re-cast to the sunken trees. The morning's stillness, which was disrupted by the sudden drama, is now as calm as before. But I'm still too close to that stinging moment of separation to be properly at ease, though I'm sure I won't lose any sleep over it. It's not like one of those tragedies from my early days, when I had less self-confidence and a whole season could pass without sight of a scale or a fin of a carp. To hook and lose one then was to experience a universal catastrophe, akin to Surrey being hit by Halley's Comet.

But, as happened once, to discover a carp in a lake that was not reputed to hold any and *then* to hook and lose it. This was beyond endurance. Now I've mentioned it I'll have to relive the whole exquisite disaster again.

During my early teens I fished an old Surrey

manor pond for tench. They were beautiful fish and more vividly green than any tench I've seen since, like highly polished green leather, but they grew to no great size and I never caught one over four pounds. It was a picturesque water, quite deep in places, surrounded by oak, pine and birch. Besides tench it held rudd, bream, perch and pike, but there were not even any rumours of carp. This surprised me as it seemed the ideal setting for some outrageously far-fetched carp epic. In fact I couldn't quite believe what the local anglers said: that there were not, nor ever had been, any carp in the pond (this was before the days when everybody denied everything). I was suspicious because the atmosphere was too much like the air that hung over the other carp waters I knew.

Just before the beginning of my second summer's tench fishing, I took a close season walk round the pond. It was a warm, settled May afternoon and I was looking forward to simply having the place to myself. I just wanted to enjoy its company without having to share it with other anglers and without bothering myself with rod and tackle. Coming round a bay towards the derelict boat house (all good carp waters should have a derelict boat house), I saw a large ripple spreading out from the crumbling brickwork. At first I thought it might really be someone mooring a boat, something that had probably not happened for half a century, but when I went and looked there was no boat and no boatman, just a slow dark swirl of water.

A phantom boat? I must have made a sudden movement for the water exploded, filling the old boathouse with spray and a big wave punched out into the bay. The surface rocked for a minute or two, then recomposed itself and was calm again. But I was in a storm because in the split second that the wave had surged across a band of sunlight I saw the biggest carp I had ever seen. Only a glimpse, yet that bright, momentary exposure fixed it indelibly in my head - dark bronze, boldly criss-crossed with large scales, blunt headed, high backed. It must have been over fifteen pounds which, at that time (1965) was stunningly huge.

The next day I was, unsurprisingly, there again, peering over the boat house wall like a cat expecting to see the mouse of its dreams. But the water was dark, unruffled and lifeless. Creeping through the bankside tunnels of rhododend-rons that occasionally opened to give narrow vignettes of the water beyond, I glimpsed several dark shadows drifting along the margins, but they were all tench. Though I spent almost the entire day looking, I didn't see another sign of that great fish, nor did I see it again during the many subsequent scoutings I made before the new season began.

But I knew it was not really necessary for me to see it again. I had discovered a wonderful secret, something only guessed at before but now known to be true. It transformed a pretty tench water into something much more dramatic and mysterious. It was a popular water which was why the fish kept itself hidden from view, but if I took time off school and went at dawn, in midweek, when no other anglers were about, I might get a chance not just of another sight, but of direct contact. The thought alone was enough to make me shudder.

First night of the season was, as I expected, an anti-climax. So many tench anglers converged on the pond that even the rudd and perch went into hiding. I went back a few days later, when that first rush-to-cast was over, and conditions were much improved. It was dull, drizzly, humid and, even

54

better, there were no other anglers present. I fished with my carp rod by the boat house and though the atmosphere was charged with anticipation all I caught was a bream. There was no suggestion, no hint that the carp might be lurking in the vicinity, in fact there were no signs for the rest of the season. The thought of hooking it may have added an extra dimension to my fishing, but I gradually began to scale down my tackle and look forward again to the mellower prospects of tench fishing. I should have guessed what was going to happen.

Nothing at all is happening here at the moment. There is still not a breath of wind on the water or in the treetops, the birds have fallen almost silent and my rod is a reassuringly static resting place for a couple of damsel flies.

I have a theory, or rather a belief, a faith in the self-fulfilling prophesy, the eventual realisation of the highly desired but extremely unlikely. If the thing you are dreaming about is potent enough to be self-sustaining once you have dreamt it and if it bears a relation to your sense of reality then, if you are patient, there is always a chance that you and it will one day cross paths. (*Casus ubique valet*, there's always a chance, is the motto of the infamous Golden Scale Club). However remote the possibility, there *is* always the chance, especially in such a chancy business as angling, that your most longed-for object of desire will become a tangible reality. The only question you need really to ask yourself is whether you'll be up to it. Will you be adequate to it or will you fall apart? There is nothing so astonishing or testing as watching the monster of your dreams materialise on the end of your line: it's as if you were thinking about conquering Everest and then find yourself miraculously on the summit, without a sherpa.

The presence of the big carp was constant. Even when I became completely immersed in my tench fishing again it was there as a deep undertone, a muted cello in an orchestra of violas. And though this was in the days before I realised the potential of the improbable, though I knew the chances of actually catching the carp were negligible, I was still more likely to succeed than any other angler simply because I knew the fish existed. However inexperienced, I was at least partly prepared and always watching for any unusual movements in the water.

Which was why, on a July morning, during my third season after tench, I suddenly noticed a cluster of bubbles on the surface different from those I'd seen before. When feeding on the bottom, the tench invariably send up little strings or patches of very small, delicate 'needle' bubbles and the bream would send up a lot of individual bubbles over a wide area. What I saw that morning was an eruption of bubbles, rising to the surface and spreading out like an expanding multi-celled amoeba. Over a year had past since I'd discovered the carp, yet it was obviously the first thing I thought of. Surely only a big carp could cause such a magnificent effervescence.

I reeled in my freelined worm and made a firm, sweeping, fluke cast that dropped the bait smack in the middle of the disturbance. Clicking over the reel pick-up I watched the line as it sank slowly towards me, then stopped sinking and remained semi-taut before rising suddenly up again, slicing audibly through the surface. Everything seemed to happen at once and the shock was almost enough to kill me. Of course I knew instantly it was no tench or bream. The tench may be strong, but it is such a placid creature that even when you're tussling gamely with it the fight is an almost leisurely affair. Bream from still waters are half asleep when you hook them and comatose when you get them ashore. The fish that grabbed my worm could surely only have been a carp, *the* carp, *my* carp.

It hauled me forward, with the rod pointing straight across the surface. The line was five pounds breaking strain and the fact that it didn't snap immediately will always be one of the world's great mysteries. The clutch on my old Intrepid Elite was set far too tight, but it suddenly gave, with a

squeal of relief and I slacked the tension screw before another crisis. I could hardly believe the size of the bow wave that romped out across the lake, in fact I could hardly believe anything that was happening. It appeared I was going through the motions of someone playing a big fish, but I was neither holding the rod nor even standing on the bank. I was somewhere else, far off, carried away by the suddenness, the almost eerie inevitability of events, unable to accept that the monster

I had spent so long thinking about was actually and over-whelmingly there.

The lake was devoid of weed and the only snags were where the bankside trees reached down into the margins. My fish went right across the lake, towards the boathouse on the east bank. Then, and surely not because of any pressure I was applying, it began to circle back towards me, throwing up wonderful furling vortices that made the water flare with silver light.

As it drew nearer I got myself back together again, imagining for the first time that, although my landing net was only eighteen inches wide, I might somehow bring the fish ashore. Closer and closer it came and I became more confident with my tackle, putting more strain on the rod and not wincing so much at the thin metallic chiming of the line.

Twenty feet out, the fish turned heavily in midwater and through the greenish depths I glimpsed a broad, black keg-shaped back. It *was* him, but I had only that one fleeting vision before it swept majestically away. The reel buzzed like a mad hornet, the rod - a Mk IV Avon - shivered in its bend, the curve beginning at the butt and ending about a yard from the tip after which the cane was parallel with the line. It seemed to lock for a moment, then stab quite violently down before whipping horribly and lifelessly straight, almost hitting me on the nose.

It was such an anticlimax, so horrible and unjust. The hook had slipped and I could do nothing more than fall on my face and bite the ground.

CHAPTER TEN

Gold

I am somewhere in the depths of the southern English countryside, yet for the past few hours I seem to have been far away not only from the cosy parochialism of this landscape but also from the rest of the world. This isn't just because of the mildly surreal nature of my immediate surroundings with their echoes of a more grandiose, romantic era, nor is it the expectation of further drama with a carp; it is mainly because of the great stillness, the peculiar quiet (now the birds are mostly silent) and the feeling that time really has wound down to a dead stop. A calm summer dawn will often have a quality of timelessness about it, but this morning it is unusually intense.

The sun has been up for almost four hours yet there is still no movement in the air, no ripple on the surface, and no sounds or signs that the ordinary world is being swept along on the usual midweek morning tide: no distant road drone or train rumble, not even the rising and falling groan of a high over-flying jet.

This is the last decade of the twentieth century.

The Secret Carp

Just 130 miles north eastward, London will be shuddering with the throb of hundreds of thousands of engines, choking in their fumes, deafened with their noise - just like yesterday and the day before that. Stepping urgently forward, yet helpless in the current of the crowd, people will be going quietly and unnoticeably crazy, their eyes on the clock, their heartbeats synchronised to the passing minutes. In a thousand other cities and towns across the country - across all the sunny side of Earth - the same incredible things are happening. But here, where the surface of the lake is an almost flawless mirror for the trees, the world is under a spell. I could, in fact, be on another planet or back in the tranquillity of a less crowded century.

You probably think I exaggerate and, to be honest, the silence is not absolute now that a few wood pigeons are cooing in close harmony over my head. There is also a willow warbler. But the stillness seems inviolate and this scene will probably remain poised in suspension until the next millenium, at least.

There is, however, the possibility that it is not the landscape which has become transfixed, but me. The mesmeric quality of the water, the hallucinatory light at sunrise and my own lack of sleep may have combined to produce a powerful sedative. My basic faculties could have deserted me and perhaps I'm unable to tell whether my surroundings really have changed during the past hour or so. Maybe it's raining, maybe a wind is blowing. Perhaps I am locked in some kind of cocoon in time and the only means of breaking out are either by making contact with a carp again or by being struck on the forehead with an aubergine.

The nice thing about sedentary carp fishing (as

opposed to active carp fishing) is that it allows you almost limitless time to abandon your conventional head for more novel modes of perception. Yet it always amazes me how quickly the senses regroup when a big fish draws near. Perhaps some

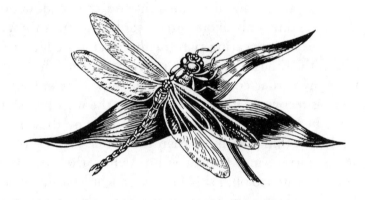

ghostly shape looms just below the surface and at first you hardly notice it. Then you realise what you had been vaguely gazing at and the jolt is like wandering into an electric fence.

I was just thinking that, as far as this morning was concerned, I had used up all the voltage this corner of the lake could generate. I was even contemplating moving my pitch, though this would have meant a monumental effort (not because I have much to carry, but because of the earth-restraining calm).

But then, out of the corner of my eye, I noticed not a deep cloudy shape but another subtler message of hope. And the messages continue, like a coded commentary on what is happening below. There. Even as I write; a lovely little blossoming of bubbles. Unlike that great eruption in the old manor pond, yet this still surely indicates that, deep down on the lake bed, a carp is truffling. They are the first bubbles I've seen today and - pause here to give thanks to Isaak - they are now rising almost directly over the bait.

It is now mid morning and the shadow of the wood is extending only about fifteen yards out across the water. The bubbles are appearing right at the shadow's edge. It must have been the thought of moving pitch that did it. The carp was aware of my earlier concentration, but now that pressure has lifted it has recovered its confidence. Like the way the fish took the bait when I was drinking my tea. But of course these jottings are really absorbing me more than the actual fishing so, if my theory is correct and fish only bite when they think your attention is switched off, I should have caught a bagful by now.

Being super-cunning, though, the carp still realised I was thinking about them and probably even knew what I was writing about. No doubt they would have liked to have interjected during certain passages, correcting mistaken assumptions. If all this is true then they know I'm now getting edgy, convinced my line is going to spill from the spool at any moment. And because of the sudden increase in concentration the fish will withdraw.

My theory is apparently flawed because there are now two separate patches of bubbles; another carp has arrived. Are they breakfasting on the corn? One feeding carp is good but two is more than twice as good because of the competition between the pair. One solitary carp can spend all day regarding a bait, but the arrival of a second fish can trigger the first into uncharacteristic decisiveness. So I'm now going to close the reel pick-up and strike at the first movement of the line ...

Ten minutes have passed and though the fish are still bubbling intermittently the line has yet to twitch. Perhaps I should gently reel in and re-bait. Maybe a small fish has whittled the corn from the hook or possibly the long submersion has washed away the natural flavour. I always think like this if the fish are feeding and nothing is happening. I convince, myself that something must be wrong, that I should have hooked one by now. I get impatient and begin to lose confidence, first in my bait, then in my presentation, then in myself.

Of course it may be that, despite what occurred earlier, the majority of these carp do not yet recognise the meaning of sweetcorn. All their lives they have sustained themselves splendidly on a wholly natural diet free from any artificial additives; then along comes an angler and offers them something that must look like a fluorescent water snail. One or two fish might be curious, the odd non-conformist may even be bold enough to roll a grain round in his mouth and it was probably one of these I hooked this morning. But the bulk of the population will simply notice something unusual - and pass on. I may try a worm in a moment. I wish I'd brought some maggots. On the other hand, what carp could refuse the gold grains?

Magnificent! I was just then staring at the place, at the edge of the shadowed water, where the bubbles were blistering the surface. There was no other blemish in the lake's smooth complexion. And then, in astonishing, almost unreal slow motion, the centre of the area I was looking at ballooned up and a great carp rose into full brilliant sunshine. It came out of the water in perfect profile nearly as far as its tail and seemed to hang at the end of its momentum for a full second, skewing slightly before sliding gracefully back into the depths. It made a big bouncing hollow in the surface which opened and closed like a pair of hands catching a ball. There was hardly any sound at all.

The fish was no monster, though it was certainly impressive - about the size of the one I lost earlier. In the strong light its scale pattern was clearly visible, but as it twisted and fell back all detail was lost in a brilliant flash of gold.

Perhaps I'll hang around here for a bit longer.

CHAPTER ELEVEN

The Curse of the Silver Pirate

Over the years, America has been an unending source of calamitous importations. You can blame Canada for its goose and India for the pheasant, but you can only blame America for the grey squirrel, the coypu, the mink, the signal crayfish, 'Dutch' elm disease, bubble gum, Elvis Presley, Kentucky Fried Chicken, Mickey Mouse, Rambo, Coca Cola, Bob Dylan and the rainbow trout. It would have been quite easy to have made this list a thousand times longer yet the last item would still have remained by far the worst.

Since the last war, the rainbow trout has become the bane of British angling. Before 1939 they used to be stocked in relatively small numbers into a few lakes and rivers, but now they are spewed in annually by the hundreds of thousands, and what with escapees from fish farms, there is hardly a river system in the country that isn't plagued by these verminous silver pirates. They have snatched my cheesepaste when I was patiently fishing for chub on the Kennet, they have gobbled my worm when I was after a barbel on the Yorkshire

The Secret Carp

Derwent, they have grabbed my breadflake when I was roach fishing on the Dorset Stour, they take everything you try to avoid them with on the Hampshire Avon and a half-pounder engulfed my size 4 Willy Gunn when I was salmon fishing on the Spey. But if I quiver with rage whenever a silver pirate beats a superior fish to my bait on a river - and even a ruffe is superior to a rainbow trout - I spout molten lava if I catch one on a carp lake.

What, we ask, are silver pirates doing in a carp lake? A more incongruous mix I couldn't imagine, like a troupe of majorettes invading a chess championship. On otherwise calm evenings they indulge in synchronised leaping, coming up like flashing cutlasses all over the lake and making it difficult - if not impossible - to discover the furtive movements of the carp. They dart at speed just below the surface and snatch at almost anything edible, which is, of course, why the rainbow trout angler offers it something that is not edible. He likes to create the illusion that this fish is difficult to catch and instead of hoicking it instantly out on a maggot or a raspberry he only uses imitation bait. And even a silver pirate is not often impressed by such whimsicality.

But you will be wondering why I have digressed so suddenly. Ten minutes after that glorious carp leapt, the line jagged once, then zipped tight. It's him! I thought. It's got to be! In the second that it took me to pick up the rod, I told myself to be firm and decisive this time and not allow the fish to get a long line on me. I struck, but instead of the expected boot-skidding haul, the rod merely shook and something frivolous went round and round in fast circles. At first I thought it must be a little carp but as I heaved it up I caught the tell-tale glint of silver.

A *pirate*! My heart, that a moment before had been expanding marvellously, suddenly sank. It was on the bank in seconds, yet though I'd tried to keep it down in the water, it insisted on thrashing wildly about and as it was nearly four pounds it resisted just long enough to effectively shatter the calm. Every carp in the lake must now be aware of my presence.

So I have four very good reasons for being in a bad mood: firstly because my long and enchanting wait ended with such a snub; secondly because I had been wound up to expect a carp at that precise moment; thirdly because the carp have now dematerialised; and fourthly because I have been reminded of the existence of silver pirates.

However, though the fuses have been glowing quite brightly they have not actually blown. Despite what I said about spouting larva, I only shouted one expletive. I am a placid person by nature and though I occasionally let myself go, I never lose my temper. And I feel much happier now I have kicked a pirate over the top of a seventy foot oak tree. No; I jest. I returned it unmolested in accordance with syndicate rules. I would certainly not have wanted to take it home for my wonderful Gaffer. She regards silver pirates in a culinary rather than piscatorial light and she has said - and I quote: 'I would rather eat bream!' (She was not talking about sea bream, either.)

CHAPTER TWELVE

A Can of Lucky Beans

The spell has definitely been broken and the day that had got stuck somewhere around the time I lost my carp, has suddenly remembered itself and begun to move on. The morning's rarified air has lifted and it now feels, looks and sounds perfectly normal. The trees are stirring overhead; new currents of air brush the lake's dark surface, sending sheets of ripple flaring across it; half a dozen small white clouds are drifting in reflection towards me, like untethered lily flowers; I can hear a tractor and a more distant engine drone. It is as if a film that had jammed in the projector had abruptly and mysteriously begun to roll again.

Now I must decide whether to stay here and hope for the carp to recover or go and fish somewhere else. Another cup of tea might help and, before I decide anything, I think I shall put all these lost carp, lost lakes and too easily found trout behind me. So far I have tuned this pen to a fairly minor key, in keeping with the mood of the morning and the various memories it evoked. Now the day has become more open and breezy I shall tune up to a more affirmative major key and we shall have fanfares and allelujias and well-bent rods. I shall go back to Redmire Pool and re-live one of those rare episodes when almost everything ...

This is very odd. As if to confirm that we have re-entered the zone of the ordinary, a man has appeared on the far bank walking his dog. Behind him scamper two children. They are the first proof since last night that homo sapiens really exists in this world. Soon they disappear down a path between trees and I have my solitude again. As I was saying, I shall relive one of those moments that help fuel the optimism of a lifetime.

July 1979 began as Julys are always meant to, hot still and clear skied. With my angling friends Barry Mills and John Carver, I was booked at Redmire for a week, but though they were at the pool from the first day - Sunday - I didn't set off until Tuesday morning.

Perfect summer weather is not always perfect for carp fishing. I like it well enough, but the carp - though always preferring warm conditions to cold - like a good breeze on the water and are even more fond of a steady drizzle, with low cloud and a muggy, close atmosphere. They dislike continuous heavy rain - or, rather, they seldom feed under these conditions. They can become listless in the de-oxygenating prelude to a thunderstorm and they can grow extremely sullen and lacklustre if the summer sky remains clear day after day and the sun burns with ever more intensity. Redmire carp in particular can seem almost paralysed by a long heatwave, which was the main reason I was in no hurry to journey to my favourite pool. In fact I even spent a couple of days finishing a photographic commission, and work has always taken second place to my more important occupation.

If nothing else, the morning of my departure was perfect for motorcycling. I put all my gear in an enormous ex-army kit bag and tied the bag to the back rack. The rods and net were slung alongside the fuel tank. I waved farewell to my lovely Gaffer at about 10 a.m. and rode off down leafy lanes, avoiding nearly all the major roads between home and Herefordshire. Stopping for lunch at an inviting-looking pub called *The Pheasant* - one of those authentic, simple country pubs that are so hard to find nowadays - I enjoyed some excellent beer and a top-of-the-range fish pie. I was also entertained by three locals who, no matter how they tried, just couldn't swing a brass ring onto a bullhorn. They were obviously practised at the game, but the ring kept missing the target.

'Come on, lads,' said the landlord. 'I'll be calling time soon.' I finished my lunch, thanked the landlord, made for the door, then paused.

'May I have a try?' I asked.

'Be our guest,' they said.

Of course I knew it was possible because I'd seen it done plenty of times before, at other pubs, and had even tried it once or twice myself. But it was still a surprise when I dropped the ring neatly over the horn first go. Someone swore, the landlord laughed and I knew I was going to catch a carp first cast. (They tried to make me do it again, but I wisely refused).

Redmire looked as lovely as ever, the water brilliantly clear and the weed growth as profuse and lush as the billowing bankside vegetation. The air was full of the pool's special perfume; a heady mix of scents from the sun-warmed water, the beds of watermint and the balsam poplars. John made me a cup of tea while he and Barry brought me up to date.

John had had a couple of chances, fishing the deeper water and Barry had achieved the remarkable feat of catching a twenty five pound mirror carp after casting from the top of a tree. But, despite this, they both complained of a general lack of piscean activity.

'I think the carp are all suffering from sunstroke,' said Barry. 'All day they were basking, semi-comatose in the weedbeds, hardly flicking a fin from dawn to dusk.'

'But what about the evenings?' I asked. 'Are they going up to the shallows then?'

'Oh yes,' they said. 'Every evening.'

So what were they complaining about? We could sleep all day and fish all night.

Sure enough, as the sun slanted into the distant Monnow valley and the shadows reached across the pool, so the carp began to stir. One by one they emerged from the clouds of waterweed and advanced towards their rich feeding grounds. With my short stalking rod and centre-pin, I crept alongside them, watching for the first one to nose down and start rooting around.

Three fish came into the green cavern beneath a great down-sweeping willow and in the shadowy margins they discovered a tasty scattering of spiced corn. My hands began to tremble as, without hesitation, the carp began to sup. I used a bit of dead twig as a float, no weight, and just a size 8 baited with three grains. Keeping my head down, I flicked out the tackle just beyond the feeding fish and, having let it settle, was about to inch it back over them when the twig, lying flat on the surface, twitched and cocked upright. It stood for a moment, then slanted away into the depths. I struck and there was the inevitable uproar as three carp made their separate exits. John came dashing down the bank thinking that, with all the commotion, I must have hooked something interesting, but after a bit of a tussle I realised I'd got the smallest of the trio - a beautiful, pert common carp of just under ten pounds. Of course I was still happy. My prediction had been correct and I was sure it was the sparkling prelude to some grand finale.

Later that night, as the moon rose, I got a carp just over ten pounds from the same spot, but then lost a much bigger fish. I wasn't however unduly ruffled as I was confident there would be numerous other chances in the days and nights to follow. At around 1 a.m. all activity suddenly ceased and I unrolled my sleeping bag, lay back under the willow and slept sublimely until after sunrise. When I woke, the mist was burning off the surface, the sky was hazy blue and, after walking quietly round the banks, I could see there wasn't a carp moving anywhere across the pool.

I spent all day lounging in the sun, swopping fishing stories with Barry and John or climbing trees to see if we could spot any carp. Most of them must have been lying deep because only a few were visible on the surface, cradled in the thickest weedbeds. They were all, though, over twenty pounds. Occasionally one of them would raise its humped back out of the water and, as if signalling or challenging, hoist its sail-like dorsal. Just for a few seconds the fin would remain erect, then fold slowly back like a rolled umbrella. Sometimes the carp would somehow flick the dorsal's front spine with an audible 'click-click', like a horse flicking its ears. (I had noticed this gesture before at Redmire and other pools and have always been mystified by it.) We tossed some of Barry's floating bait at them but they showed no interest in anything, except basking. Not until about eight o'clock in the evening did they gently push out of the fronds and drift into open water.

At first only a small congregation began the pilgrimage to the shallows, but then, as the sun sank lower, an extraordinary procession appeared. In the midst of this slowly advancing column was, without doubt, the largest carp in Britain. It dwarfed all the monsters I'd ever seen before and would have stupefied even the most hard-bitten angling sceptic. It could have given a casual passer-by heart failure. Over four feet long, it was perfectly proportioned and could not have weighed less than seventy pounds.

I have written about this phenomenal encounter elsewhere and apologise for repeating myself, but it was one of the great moments of my angling life. I'll say no more, except to add that this was the only time I clearly saw the real giant of Redmire and I think I knew the place better than anyone. Once, when I was drifting in the punt, I saw something enormous explode out of one weedbed and vanish into another. All I could swear to on that occasion was that it was a common carp and it was colossal, but it may not have been the king. (After it had sunk away, I hung over the side of the punt staring down into the depths, and noticed, after a while, that my loudly beating heart was causing a thin ripple to pulse out across the surface.)

Naturally, I fished with a tense uncharacteristic concentration through the evening and into the night, but never had the merest tug of a response. Yet the shallows were boiling with feeding fish. Even in the dark I could see the water going pale with stirred up mud. It was obviously time for the carp

to reap some rich harvest of larvae, but their minds were tuned
only for that and not for the kind of confectionary I was offering.

John and Barry, fishing the deeper water,
experienced less drama and similarly slack lines, but I was still
surprised when, at breakfast the next morning, Barry suddenly

announced his decision to leave. Though more of a realist than
me, Barry is still an optimist - and a great angler - but nothing
had touched his baits for three days and he said, what with the
continuing heatwave, he didn't rate his chances any longer.
Naturally, he was still mighty pleased with his one big fish.

After he'd gone, John and I took the punt out for a
spot of carp gazing. We drifted over the dense and marvellous
forests of weed, waiting for the moment when some deep-lying
fish would notice our presence and lunge away, making the long
feathery streamers of hornwort writhe and twist, like a typhoon
in the Amazon. During the course of our voyage several large

holes whirled open in the weedbeds, but though we drifted down the entire length of the pool we only clearly saw one fish - a rapidly-departing twenty pound mirror carp. It was another very hot day and we had expected to be drifting quietly amongst dozens of basking fish, as we had often done before. However, we were not particularly surprised. While Redmire can sometimes flaunt its treasures almost brazenly, it can also conceal them utterly - often for no apparent reason. We paddled back to the dam, still peering over the side but all we saw was a playful shoal of gudgeon.

Nothing moved across the pool all day, but I was not concerned, especially when, in mid-afternoon, a westerly breeze sprang up, texturing the surface with ripples. There had hardly been a movement of air all that week and the oxygenating wind, blowing straight up the pool, would obviously prick up a few carp scales.

As expected, the fish were on the move some hours before sunset, visible as grey ghosts under the ripples, all converging on the shallows again. Several of them skirted the outer branches of the willow, where I'd taken the other fish and, using a blowpipe, I managed to get a bait through a four-inch gap in the trailing leaves into the open water beyond. Then I sprinkled a few free grains around it. My plan was simple: Hook an obviously unsuspecting fish, dive in, wade through the dense curtain of leaves and branches and play the carp out from the middle of the shallows. I so nearly succeeded.

After only a few minutes an impressive sheet of bubbles fizzed to the surface, directly over the bait. Furthermore, they were individually big bubbles and at Redmire the size of the bubble is often in proportion to the size of the carp. Within seconds the line drew steadily taut. I flicked the rod up and the water beyond the willow lifted into a bright dome that didn't quite explode, but bulged smoothly and slowly away to the left.

The apparition of the previous night immediately sprang to mind and as I plunged into the water I had a wild idea that it was there again but this time on the end of my line. Completely unstoppable, almost casual in its majestic, whale-like progress, it swung out towards the centre of the shallows. A knot or a kink snatched horribly against the willow fronds and before I could get the rod through the gap the line sprang suddenly from one side to the other as the fish turned and accelerated up the pool. A wave went past as big as the front end of an express train. Then the line jammed in a forked twig and it was as if someone had gripped my throat. There was a ghastly pause, a muffled crack and the broken line sprang back round the rod tip. I sloshed ashore, chewing the sleeves off my shirt.

Even the most glorious hours have their darker moments and this turned out to be rather a black Friday. But then hardly any stay at Redmire was without at least one visitation from a line-tangling, foot-tripping little demon. I threw out another scattering of corn into the more open water to one side of the tree and followed it up with a hookbait. Soon the carp had recovered from the disturbance and were on the groundbait, bubbling like frogs. When they stopped, another handful of corn got them going again.

Moments before sunset I had a slow deliberate take and struck a fish which hung almost motionless in midwater before surging off down the pool. John came running up with the net and after seeing the size of the departing bow wave, agreed with me that it was 'quite a big fish'. It plunged into a weedbed halfway across to the islands on the far bank, then rolled heavily and turned to my left. With the cane hooped into a wonderful bend I brought the carp to a swirling halt and was just wondering whether I should go wading again, to keep the line clear of overhanging branches, when the hook popped out.

Within half an hour, when it was almost dark, every carp had vanished. The breeze still hissed in the willows and the pool glimmered under a clouded moon.

Just before sunrise there was the awful sound of a wardrobe falling into the water. Before the reverberations had died away several smaller cupboards and a chest of drawers also crashed through the surface. A few minutes' deep silence followed and I turned in my bed and wondered what on earth was going on. Why was the furniture toppling into the pool? And why could I not wake up properly? Suddenly a bookcase lurched forward and the entire contents cascaded from the shelves with a great, stuttering splash.

'Whoa!' I shouted, and sat up to find myself in my sleeping bag under the willows, with about fifty carp crashing through the margins next to me.

They were spawning. The uproar was quite unbelievable and had obviously been going on for some time. It had been several years since I'd last witnessed the Redmire nuptials and I'd forgotten just how wild an occasion it was. The entire shallows were one great unfurling cloud of pinkish mud and the margins had been whipped into a froth as the carp chased one another under the line of willows, gradually working down towards the deeps. They cavorted, tumbled and walloped away from me like a receding thunderstorm.

I rubbed my eyes into proper focus, lit my camping stove and made myself a cup of tea. The sky was full of broken cloud and though the breeze had dropped it seemed as if the weather was definitely on the turn. I had just one more full day's fishing and what I needed to boost my confidence was another warm wind accompanied by a great downpour. If the clouds closed and thickened perhaps my prayers would be answered, but of course the carp would have to stop spawning as well.

Over a second cup of tea, down by the dam, John told me that even if he hadn't already planned to leave Redmire that same day, the spawning fish would have persuaded him to pack his gear.

'They've already spawned once, a fortnight ago,' he said. 'When they've finished this time they'll lie doggo for a week.'

As we sipped our tea, we watched the weedbeds in front of us erupt with an orgy of carp. Yet, despite the commotion, it didn't appear as if the whole population had joined in the throng. It was not as furious a party as the one I'd witnessed before.

I helped John carry some of his gear round to his car, we said our goodbyes and he drove slowly away.

'See you here in August!' I shouted after him.

The clouds did not continue to build, in fact they lifted and merged into one silvery blanket through which the sun dimly shone. A warm, steady breeze began to blow from the west again. By noon the spawning had finished and one or two fish even began to move up onto the shallows to feed - the earliest this had happened all week. I hadn't normally begun to fish until late evening, but on that particular Saturday I had my first cast after lunch.

Carp ghosted close to my willow again, but seemed aware of my presence and turned up their noses at the sweetcorn. I moved up the bank a little and tried again, but the fish ignored even my free offerings. I would have to try something else.

At the bottom of my bag was a very old can of Smedley's broad beans. I had only used beans twice before at Redmire; initially they were extremely effective, but the carp had not responded to them at all afterwards. Conditions that first time were uncannily similar to the day in question with fish suddenly moving onto the shallows in the afternoon. So I opened the can and went right up to the top of the pool, creeping onto the little alder-shaded island near the feeder stream. I had to inch into casting position with all the exaggerated stealth of a stalking heron as there were over a dozen big fish quietly browsing within a few feet of me. I baited the hook and gently cast towards one of the largest carp, checking the line in mid-flight so that the bean landed like a leaf just in front of him. He disregarded it and carried on sifting for larvae.

I tossed in a few free offerings and then had to recast as drifting weed, shifted by the breeze, dragged against the line. Several fish swam towards me from further down the pool and though one carefully inspected the bait the others seemed quite wary of it and avoided it. The free beans were likewise left severely alone. At least the carp didn't appear to be aware of my presence. Faintly at first, but then more clearly, the sound of church bells came down the breeze from the local village. I took that as a good omen.

A Can of Lucky Beans

I re-baited with the smallest bean in the can and just lowered it into the water below the rod tip. After a few minutes a pair of twenty pound commons came ponderously into view from my right, skirting round the island. The larger of the two passed right beneath me, moving with an easy confidence that made my bones crackle in anticipation. With hardly a pause, he scooped up the bean and mooched on. The line swung in behind him, cutting gently through the surface film.

All around me were sunken brambles and sprouting willow shoots and in the split second before striking I tried to guess which snag he'd make for first. I jagged the rod to the right and there was an amazing swirl and a sound like the water being hit by a cricket bat. With a ferocious lunge, the carp turned and disappeared back round the island. I was using a Mk IV carp rod and an Ambidex loaded with ten pound line, yet I could do no more than simply hang on as the fish ripped down the centre of the shallows. And because the island tree was hanging across the line I had no alternative but to jump in and follow (incredibly, I had enough presence of mind not to forget my net). I floundered along in the carp's wake, like a heavily-laden shopper trying to catch up with a bus. The bed of the pool was, however, surprisingly firm and only once did I stumble into a silt pit. By clamping down on the reel I simply let the carp pull me out again.

I didn't stop wading until I was well clear of the worst snags and had reached a point almost level with my original pitch by the big willow. Standing waist deep in the centre of the shallows, I wound down and tried to convince the fish that it was time for a closer understanding. There was a great thumping splash as he dived into a distant weedbed, but the weed was thick and I knew he'd get no further. I began to retrieve a few turns of line and he suddenly burst out of his sanctuary and ploughed towards the right-hand bank, where a willow was leaning into the margins. Laying the rod over and firmly increasing pressure, I was only just able to steer him away from disaster.

Though the disturbance had naturally driven all the other fish from the shallows, after about three or four minutes I was astounded by the sight of a bow wave coming back level and then past me as a carp returned to the feeding grounds. Others followed, seemingly indifferent to my presence or the plight of their companion.

Gradually I worked my carp towards me and he swung left and then right again, materialising suddenly beneath the surface, looking very dark and impressive. He was not impressed with me at all and made another terrific whirl of water, turning and sweeping powerfully away again. I managed to slow and stop him and he glowered on the bottom, trying to anchor me in a sparse weedbed. A moment's impasse followed.

Then everything became animated once more and I knew it was time to prepare the net. I leant the handle against my shoulder with the mesh slanting underwater, then got both hands back to the rod again and began easing the fish towards me. There were pennants of silky weed all along the line which began to slide together as they were drawn in. I lifted the rod high to clear them and a great green banner rose up through the surface. It wouldn't shake free, though as it dripped water it lost weight and became less of a problem. I still didn't like it, because eventually it jammed up against the top ring and felt horribly cumbersome.

The fish plunged not more than fifteen feet from me and only then, when I saw it really clearly, did I suddenly

realise how my right arm was aching and how dry my throat had become. He turned on a short line, every detail of him blazing through the water. There was a tight knot of weed attached close to the hook and when he turned it pressed against his flank and I could feel it rubbing awkwardly. He looked bigger than I first estimated, moreover his appearance was so splendid, so exquisite that if at that stage of the encounter he'd suddenly departed he could have caused a death by drowning. (The coroner gave a verdict of suicide caused by the loss of a great fish).

There was another crunching explosion of water and another wide, outspreading wave. The clutch snarled a little, then I quietly coaxed the fish back for the final approach. He came almost resignedly over the mesh, but when I tried to lift the net it hardly moved. It was too deep down and, with just my left hand, I couldn't bring it up fast enough. Curse the micromesh, I thought, and did something completely stupid and very nearly disastrous. I let go of the rod and, with the carp just beginning to turn on the surface, got both hands to the net handle and heaved, bringing the mesh up, up until the fish was completely out of the water and the handle was bending dangerously.

The ripples spread away and I remained standing for some minutes, half submerged, wholly elated, staring down at the beautiful sleek form in the mesh. It looked like a golden milk churn. Sloshing ashore onto the west bank, I laid the fish gently amongst reeds, still cradled in the net and went to fetch my camera and spring balance. After I'd weighed him and taken his portrait, I apologised for disrupting his afternoon and released him. He cruised off serenely, threading his way into a deep jungle of weed. Twenty seven pounds, six ounces he weighed: a male common. Of course there is nothing sensational about a carp that size from Redmire, yet this particular specimen was not only extremely handsome, it appeared at a moment that could not have been more perfect. It shall always be one of my most memorable fish.

I put the kettle on and, while it was simmering, changed out of my sodden clothes. Clean, dry socks were almost as welcome as a cup of tea. Then I went for a walk to think about the strangeness of fishing. I passed the old black barns by the feeder stream and walked up the hay field on the edge of the valley. The skylarks were singing, the amber clouds were like flags at a victory parade and the church bells were still ringing in Langarren.

CHAPTER THIRTEEN

The Secret Carp

It must be about noon. The sun is not only at its highest point of the day but also at its highest point of the year, almost directly overhead. Yet I am still in dappled shade. All the reflections were blown away an hour ago and now there is a steady building-up of sound as the breeze rises, just as it did yesterday (and just as it did on that lovely day at Redmire). The ripples are hurrying down to the dam and the occasional cloud floats swiftly across the sky. I have cast and re-cast several times, but there has been no more response from the fish (or, thank Isaak, from the trout).

There has been no sight or sign of fish either, though, remembering Redmire, this shouldn't worry me. If the carp in that small pool could seemingly disappear for days on end then the fish here could conceal themselves for years. This lake is ten times the size of Redmire; what chance, then, of finding a carp that's feeling sullen? More interestingly, what chance of discovering any individual monster?

It was many years since I had that one staggering

87

view of the Redmire King and I spent more time watching the water than fishing. Though there were, over the last thirty years, several other fishermen privileged with a clear sight of Leviathan, to the majority of Redmire anglers it was just another myth - a myth which some people found amusing, some found inspiring and others found absurd.

Though I've often been accused of exaggerating I present the King as a historical fact. Better men than me saw it and all agreed that it was more than simply extraordinary. But no-one but me can compare it so accurately to a fifty-pounder and therefore say just how much bigger it was. It must have been (*been?* perhaps it still exists) the largest carp in Great Britain, possibly the biggest in Europe, and yet its domain was just a three acre pool.

However, just as the King was an authentic mystery there is almost certainly another aristocarp - though obviously not such a big one - living in secret seclusion down some deep drowned valley under this lake. The fish I saw yesterday was probably one of his courtiers.

A heron almost crash-dived into the water just then as he twisted and swooped to avoid the beaks of two pursuing crows. He was quietly rowing through the air, looking for a peaceful place to fish and two black phantoms just dropped out of the sky onto his head.

It must be true that virtually every carp water in the country has its own monster story and whether based on fact or not, every tale lends something to the atmosphere of a place. This is all fine and dandy, even when the 'monster' turns out to be no bigger than five pounds. But when the monster of the myth is *truly* monstrous, it invariably overshadows and obscures the more accessible pleasures of carp fishing. Talk of the giant generates an onslaught by dozens of over-equipped anglers and, suddenly, every lesser carp is regarded with contempt.

I am talking here about an outsize fish that has been seen but not caught, yet, puzzlingly, there are many anglers travelling the rounds of the country's carp waters specifically for

big carp that *have* been caught before. They hear that an outstanding fish has been landed and returned and so deliberately undertake to repeat history and recapture the same specimen.

In waters where fish are fairly easy to catch, a particular giant can feel the inside of a landing net half a dozen times a season and it's a moment of triumph when someone lands a big fish that is unfamiliar. The whole spirit of carp fishing surely becomes lost under those circumstances; everything becomes mechanical, repetitive, predictable and ultimately mundane.

I know I can be accused of catching the same carp more than once. My own record fish ended up twice in my net, but there was a seven year gap between captures and it grew thirteen pounds heavier during that time.

Much of my disenchantment with carp fishing began in the early 80s. Not only was there an increasingly cheerless, emotionless, macho attitude on the banks, with fishermen becoming more selfish, competitive and unbearably earnest, there was also a revolution in carp fishing techniques, with anglers going to the most dubious lengths to outwit the fish.

Some of these tricks were clever and innovative, but on many lakes they were just too clever and the fish became ridiculously easy to catch. Suddenly I could sympathise with the attitude of the trout angler, with his eccentric imitation baits. He doesn't wish to make things too easy and knows that his kind of fishing will endure simply because he has incorporated so many elements of skill and watercraft into it. Carp fishing is heading in the opposite direction.

However well educated a fish, if it lives in an overcrowded, hungry water and is presented with a bait on ultra-fine nylon, it will take that bait almost every time. Tiddler-snatchers always hooked more carp than carp anglers. One of the new tricks was to attach a few inches of thin line to the end of a hook which was, in turn, attached to a standard high breaking strain carp line. The bait was cunningly threaded onto the end of the ultra-fine nylon. This was the 'hair-rig' and though initially very successful, the carp eventually began to see the point of it: yet I objected to it from the very beginning and I object even more now, when all kinds of fiendish alternatives are appearing on the market.

The Secret Carp

One I read about recently had two tiny hooks on the fine line so that the bait would 'snag' in the carp's mouth and prevent the fish from ejecting it. All a modern carp angler has to do nowadays is cast out, go to sleep and then reel in when his bite indicator sounds. There is no more timing of the strike or anything so comically subtle. As a specialist pursuit, carp fishing is comparatively new, and has only been widely established for about forty years. It was always regarded as the most demanding and exciting branch of angling, and yet nowadays, on many waters, it is about as exciting and demanding as playing snap with a tortoise.

It always amused me to watch the way any successful or proven item of tackle was immediately adopted and accepted as a standard requirement by carp anglers. But now this standardisation has gone beyond a joke. Not only do the majority of carp anglers have to fish with at least three identical rods and reels, they must also have the complete product range of whoever happens to be the most fashionable tackle and bait manufacturers of the day. And of course they also require waters that can accommodate this multi-rodded, heavily equipped regimental approach. So the lakes have become standardised as well. Ultimately, even the fish have become standardised with all specimens entered onto graphs which show growth ratios, condition factors, identification marks, colour variations, dietary habits, intelligence ratings, dress sense, musical appreciation and knowledge of world history.

Only the rank beginner can really enjoy this game for he doesn't have to appear to know what he's doing, doesn't have to own a battery of rods and a supply depot and doesn't mind showing his true emotions when his first carp tumbles into the net. For the experienced angler, however, there are no more surprises and no more secrets. Everything has been reduced to the known and the ordinary.

Of the scores of letters I get every year from anglers, one of the predominant themes is the lamentable state of carp angling across the country. Ignore it, I say, carry on and enjoy yourself in your own way. But then I get replies like this:

'Returned to my favourite water and began to fish a formerly productive swim hidden between thick beds of reed mace. Imagine the shock when - one, two, three - three great leger leads whistled over from the far bank, a hundred yards away, and crashed into the margins near my rod tip. Every carp in the area dived for cover! I'm not joking. The culprit must have been using quarter pound leads! Apart from the unbelievable wallop when they hit the water, imagine if he'd overcast or snapped off. I would have been found, days later, with a hole straight through my skull! I can't go back again. Apart from the disturbance, which made the fishing pointless, it's too bloody dangerous.'

This encouraged me to have a look in the angling magazines and see what was on offer from the specialist tackle trade. It was hilarious and appalling, with specifically designed carp fishing leads up to *six* ounces, the sort of weight you might require fishing for halibut in the North Sea. Yet slightly more perplexing than the missiles themselves were their names: *Cruise, Cluster, Patriot* and *Buzz Bombs*, all redolent of that morose Rambo tendency that has already given us a rod called the *Armalite Top Gun*. Even now the military-angling complex is probably dreaming of the *Uzzi* bait sprayer, the *Kalashnikov* stalking rod and, for those iced-up lakes in deepest winter, the

Napalm bomb. These would be the hot favourites if you were a genuine flak-jacketed carp squaddie. After all, it isn't fishing any more, it's war.

When the world was young, when the sun was your friend and telephones had bells, when cars stopped after they'd run you over and an angler dreamed of catching a single carp in a lifetime, I had this pleasant image of a typical club carp water: the banks were well-trodden but still green and overgrown and the margins were hazardous with snags, from lily beds to old bicycles. There would always be a couple of semi-permanent 'experts' fishing intently in the place where, ten years before, a visitor once landed a ten pounder; a father and son would be float fishing in a sunny corner and a few youngsters would be trying desperately to get a bite from a six-inch crucian carp; now and then, from the densest weed beds, a great fish would rocket into the air and everyone, including the experts, would look up and gasp. But now the world and the carp lake has changed.

Today there is a grim encirclement of rods and each regularly positioned fishing platform looks like a gun emplacement, what with the nylon domes and the bristling carbons mounted on stainless steel 'rod pods'. No anglers are actually visible, even though there isn't much natural cover on the banks, they are all in their bivvies watching their transistor televisions and drinking lager; the electronic bite alarms echo across the water, sounding like a computer stuttering towards self-destruct.

It is this general air of falsity which I find so baffling, this feeling that the whole marvellous point of the fishing has become lost under a welter of purely technical considerations regarding tackle, bait and unneccessary paraphernalia. The concentration on efficiency and results means that all the modern carp angler requires is a hole in the ground stocked with artificially-reared, force-fed monsters that he can catch again and again. No wonder so many veteran carp fishers are turning to other things - like gudgeon snitching.

Yet across the country there *are* still marvellous pools that have somehow remained unnoticed by the squaddies and the machine minders, and there will always be a few lakes like this one, where the depths still have their mysteries and the carp still have their secrets.

CHAPTER FOURTEEN

A Dip of the Float

Early afternoon and instead of the deep soporific stillness I was expecting, it seems we are building for a storm. I was looking forward to a short post-lunch siesta, but it would be difficult to sleep when the world seems on the verge of a stampede. Everything's seething, and roaring. The vegetation round my feet is flickering like green fire, the oak above is swaying majestically and the wood behind me sounds like an ocean. There is also a gigantic cloud rising up from the north west and though a long way off - maybe ten miles - there is no doubt that this lake is directly in its path. My hat blew off while I was eating my tuna sandwich. Then it blew off again when I was drinking my tea and now it's anchored on the ground with a stone.

When I think of all the carp I've taken in conditions like this, fishing into the teeth of a rising wind, I can't believe I'm not going to catch one now. I'm positive the fish are moving closer and can almost feel their approach, like a dowser senses the proximity of a subterranean stream. Three times the line has jumped taut, though there's never been enough afterdraw for me to respond to. But the minutes tick past, the cloud draws nearer and I'm now wondering whether the fish I hooked this morning wasn't even more of a fluke than normal. I can't even make any more tea. The wind is blowing straight across to this corner of the lake and I'd need a flamethrower to get the kettle going. No! It's no good. This is too frustrating and I'm going to have to scout along the bank and see if I can't find a fish to cast to ...

Two things have happened. Firstly, the wind has dropped abruptly, just as if someone had closed an enormous door to stop the draught, and secondly, I have found not just one, but almost a dozen carp. They are still here, not thirty feet away from me as I write.

The whole lake has begun to smooth out into an uneasy, gently heaving and billowing calm, a kind of trembling recovery. But though the reflections have yet to re-form on the surface I can see clearly the dark shapes of the fish as they patrol to and fro along the edge of a big patch of lilies. The bed stretches along the margins for about twenty five yards and spreads twenty feet into the lake. I'm sure the carp haven't noticed me here, shrouded as I am with dense foliage and shaded by a towering chestnut. The tree rears up out of the water, its snaking roots making a secure sanctuary for any hooked fish.

The carp are not all in sight, but there are, as I said, about a dozen, ranging in weight from five to around fifteen pounds. Previous observation convinces me that the fish in this lake are not even curious about surface baits, but the carp here are cruising actively near the top therefore I'm using a favourite lily bed tactic and fishing a float with the bait suspended just below the surface on the far side of the pads. The red-tipped quill is almost perfectly stationary and actually touching one of the lily leaves. And, to add to the excitement (I am absurdly confident), the leaves give an occasional lurch as a fish barges between them.

Perhaps, though, the fish are only active because they are anxious, suspicious of the unexpected stillness. Suddenly the sun is blotted out. The great sulphur-coloured cloud is now filling half the sky, but the carp remain near the surface, even though they must realise this is the lull before the storm. Maybe I should try and switch my mind off the fish and consider the cloud instead.

As the cloud-forming currents of air spiral upwards they will, if they are strong enough, form a gigantic lung which sucks in the air from miles around and will, as obviously happened here, even rein back the prevailing wind. A thundercloud - there is a carp right next to the float, which quivers as he shadows past - a thundercloud will often advance, growing all the time until it is so mountainous it can hardly move and remains stationary, like my float now. I thought this might be a thundercloud but there've been no ominous rumbles, it isn't as intimidating - the float moved then a few inches to the right. Pen-down time ...

To register my euphoria I have just tried to draw a straight line across the page. Its laughable crookedness proves there's been a bit of a splash. I've caught a carp and it's as if I'd just landed the fish of a lifetime, I'm so pleased about it. Yet it's hardly prodigious, probably no more than ten pounds. Indisputably splendid, though, and my first from this lake.

The quill had slid to the right, then it was still for

a moment. I picked up the rod and the float dipped almost to the last quarter-inch of its red tip. I was just going to strike, when it rose an inch and finally set off at half cock across the surface. Unmissable, and the strike connected me to a fish that drove down deep, then flashed like lightning round to the right, shooting straight towards the chestnut roots. Remembering the earlier loss I piled on as much sidestrain as I dared and the carp curved in towards me and almost hit the bank. It somersaulted and I saw the gold of the scales before it dived again and ploughed straight out into the lilies, dragging the pads under in its wake. It stuck solidly; but steady, patient pressure finally uncorked it and it came sloshing to the surface, wallowing, rolling and flopping into the waiting net.

There was almost certainly a colony of original wild carp in this lake and my fish is one of the descendants, with a long, streamlined body, small head and seemingly over-large fins and tail. Because of the presence of king carp it may not be pure bred and yet it has all the wildie's more graceful characteristics. It is lying in the net as I write, stirring in the shallow water by my feet. I will release it in just a moment, after this attempt at a word portrait.

He's a noble-looking specimen, elegant and yet powerful, like a more compact version of a barbel. His length must be about twenty six inches. The back, when seen out of the water, is ultramarine blue merging quickly into the glistening bronze of the flank which, in turn, pales into a rich yellow ochre along the belly. Around the head is a mottling of grey, turquoise and amber and there is an iridescent flaring across the gills like the inside of an oyster shell. The whole head, in fact, is like a grooved and ribbed shell, an armoured

A Dip of the Float

cowling out of which the jet black eye, rimmed with gold, perpetually stares. The gill plates are slowly pulsing, re-energising the carp with oxygen and the lips are faintly moving, as if whispering an incantation (or a curse), like the mouth of a pouting buddha. The fins and tail are midnight-blue tinged with crimson and they move and furl like a cloak billowing in a wind. Along the flank each exquisitely aligned scale reflects the sky.

CHAPTER FIFTEEN

A Nose for Water

As the years pass I get more and more dubious about my angler's obsession with statistics and closer to the day when I shall toss my spring balance into the lake. However, I confess that I carefully weighed my fish and was slightly miffed that it didn't quite make ten pounds. A nine and three quarter pound wildie is a fine sounding specimen - the equivalent to a twenty pound king carp - but a double-figure wildie sounds even finer.

I relaunched the fish and it blurred quickly into the dark underneath the lily pads, leaving a vortex coiling like a signature on the surface. It also left its distinctive smell on my hands, a smell that is sharp and peppery, almost, as I said before, like herbs and marmalade. A carp does not become properly real until you have touched it and smelt it and the odour of carp, especially now, at the beginning of a new season, is as evocative as the smell of the sea.

Scents are difficult to describe, yet the memory records nothing so precisely. They are stored deep and are forgotten sometimes for years or even decades until, suddenly, you catch again the exact equivalent and are instantly taken back in time - to a barn where you played when you were ten, or to a hospital that seemed a long way from home, or to a toy cap gun, or the perfume of your first girlfriend. Fishing is full of unique and diverse pockets of air, from the delicious sweetness of a river on a summer night to the whiff of vintage mould rising from an old creel. There is, in fact, no occupation except gardening that I appreciate as much through the nose as the eyes. At this time of the year the waterside air can seem more sumptuous than a tropical greenhouse, but then there are other associated smells even more pungent than a compost heap.

I remember once travelling across Ireland with Nick in the back of a small van. It was hot and humid and we almost died because we were sitting next to several steaming keepnets reeking of congealed bream slime. More powerful than this was another Irish aroma, the nose-curling stink of smouldering bones wafting from a riverside glue factory. The outfall of this place had become a prolific big fish swim but the stench was almost blinding, like the corrosive cloud above an acid bath. Of course an angler with a desire for a monster fish can overcome any hindrance and we fished the entire day with scarves tied tightly round our faces.

The sweetest-smelling water I know is undoubtedly Redmire Pool, mainly because of the pervasive perfume of the big balsam poplars, but there are other subtler, yet equally delectable airs hovering about the place. In mid summer these are all tinged with the actual smell of carp and during the approach to spawning there is an unmistakable fishy musk which can become quite penetrating and almost sickly.

A Nose for Water

Rivers, especially chalkstreams, have a lighter more delicate 'nose' than still waters, like a crisp white wine, while little overgrown field ponds exhale a pleasant yeasty air that I always associate with the wholesome smell of tench. Every different species has its own individual scent though many, like the roach, dace and chub, are virtually indistinguishable. The grayling has always been famous for smelling like thyme, while a salmon smells like freshly cut rhubarb. Brown trout have a softer, mildly fruity scent and barbel smell like raw potatoes seasoned with lemon juice (don't tell the fish and chip trade!). Apart from the minnow, which can smell like liver, the sweetest-smelling fish are the smallest, the bullhead, loach and gudgeon; while the most malodorous are stillwater bream, which remind me of manure. Eels are not unpleasant and pike, unsurprisingly, are like a mashed compound of them all.

One of my favourite angling smells is the warm treacly smell of a freshly-varnished cane rod and I recently had a new rod made for me that smelt like vintage brandy. Before the advent of nylon I used to like the smell of newly waterproofed nets and the interior of every angling shop used to be heavy with it, intermixed with the odours of canvas, waxed coats, varnish, linseed oil, aniseed, sawdust, maggots and rubber boots.

Nowadays gas masks are advisable before entering some tackle shops, so permeated are they with the nauseous cloud rising from factory-made baits, flavours and additives - almost all of them produced for carp fishing. The list of 'bait enhancers' is simply nose-boggling and supremely comic; everything from fermented krill to peach melba, from Japanese oyster extract to Madagascar basil. Together with the overwhelming and almost explosive cocktail of bottled chemical-additives - everything from phosphorous to pantothenic acid - these bizarre and baffling garnishings make the modern tackle shop smell like a cross between Willy Wonka's Chocolate Factory and Dr. Frankenstein's kitchen.

Of course fishermen smell, too, especially damp fishermen. There is, for instance, a magnificent piquancy about a coach-load of anglers travelling home after a rainsoaked and successful day on the river. But the most evocative and irresistible scent of all is the smell of a lakeside in summer after a heavy fall of rain. It is a fragrance I shall be savouring within the hour.

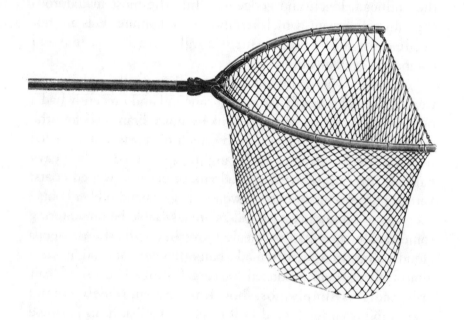

CHAPTER SIXTEEN

Hercules and the Storm

The sky has become quite dark with cloud and there is a wonderfully eerie silence. The lake gleams like steel and the trees look unreal in the distance - clearly defined yet somehow fragile and precarious before the storm, like bottles in a shooting gallery. And there *is* going to be a storm because I can see the cloud base being torn down by an almost invisible column of rain that can't be more than two miles away. Though the birds have been subdued by the lowering of pressure there isn't that oppressive airlessness that often presages a thunderstorm. I think there will only be the rain.

I am back in my original pitch, having hurried along the bank so that I could unfurl my battered brolly. There's also an ex-army gas cape in case things get serious and naturally I've put my hat back on. Though I've re-cast it's doubtful whether the carp will stir until the storm passes over. I have rarely caught many carp during a downpour, yet their enthusiasm in the steaming aftermath can be impossible to cope with. There can be so many fish galvanised by sudden hunger that it's sometimes difficult to decide where to cast.

But here it comes. Gradually the most distant line of trees disappears behind a grey curtain that draws silently across the width of the lake and seems to glide more swiftly as it approaches. Faintly I begin to hear a sound, like an off-station radio slowly being turned up in volume. The dark surface shrinks towards me as the rain advances, flailing the lake to silver. Even as I write, the sound of it rises from a whisper to a hissing rasp and now a roar. An astounding deluge cascades over my head. The brolly shudders, it sounds like gravel falling on it, yet I'm partially protected by overhanging boughs. It's so loud and tumultuous I have to laugh. The individual raindrops are the same shape and almost as large as light bulbs. They seem to fall slowly, yet at a rate of millions per second and each one makes a big brief bubble when it hits the water. The ground behind me looks as if it's smoking and the spray is making blots all across my page. Yet, with all this violence and disruption, nothing is being destroyed except the dust. It mixes into a thick foaming broth that gives off the most delicious scent in the world.

I can't see further than about fifty yards and if I got out from under this brolly I'd have to swim. Surely it can't keep up this intensity for long? Just before I ran back here I had again been imagining a comfortable place to curl up in, but there are now no comfortable places and anyway the fish will soon be roused into a corn-chomping frenzy. Also, there is nothing like a cold shower to shock you awake. However, I think this one might outstay its welcome. The entire sky has become drawn down and there's no optimistic glow in the north-west. I shall simply have to sit it out.

I remember another storm in a situation almost identical to this, but with the added spice of thunder. I was tench fishing at Frensham Little Pond, just a few miles from my old home. The sky had been full of white cumulus all morning, though lurking near the horizon were dark storm clouds the colour of ash. They'd been sailing harmlessly from west to east but, after the fifth lovely tench had taken my float down, I noticed a boiling thunderhead rising suddenly from the north, across the direction of the prevailing wind. I missed a bite as I watched closely to see if it really was coming my way and not just billowing. But like today's vaporous monster, it was going to hit me amidships.

Low murmurings rose to a continual threatening rumbling, then its great black hood rose across the sun and it was time to go. Foolishly, I had no protective gear - not even a waterproof jacket - and there was nowhere on the vast heath for me to shelter. Moreover, I only had my bicycle, an ex-police Hercules, circa 1911.

I don't think I've ever packed my gear so fast, not even when I was late for a strawberry tea. Strapping my creel to the back-rack and shouldering the holdall, I set off at speed along the narrow, sandy paths. Behind me, the rumbling was growing into a more substantial jaw-trembling boom and at the top of a little rise I just had to stop and look back. It was a phenomenal sight. Beyond a line of pine trees on the pond's far bank was an immense purple wall of cloud and the rain falling from it looked like the smoke of a forest fire.

As I stared, fascinated, there were three deadly stabs of lightning, two behind the trees and then one directly into the pond. The thin crack as it hit the water made me flinch and the immediately succeeding crash of thunder almost bowled me over. In the midst of the thumpings and boomings a brief but violent wind began to blow and the pond's surface, that had been calm, was suddenly full of racing waves, like horses stampeding across acres of glass.

Exactly as I saw just now, the distant tree-line dissolved in the oncoming rain, but the light was brighter so it looked less like a grey curtain and more like an enormous silver blade scything over the landscape. Though its progress appeared laboured, I fled away across the heath, pedals blurring. The old ironwork made some terrific noises as Hercules and I hurtled down sandy slopes, rattled across tree roots, and cranked up hills. But the storm, pounding and crunching behind me, was closing fast and an anxious glance over my shoulder told me I'd never make it. It now looked like a tidal wave about to break over my head. My lungs were ready to burst and the rather dry chain was jumping badly on the worn rear sprocket.

There was another bright flash followed straight away by a volcanic roar. I wavered in mid-pedal, then churned on, hearing through the thunder the rush of the approaching rain. If I could go at twenty miles per hour, the storm was going at thirty, and while I zig-zagged along winding paths and crawled up steep inclines, its progress was constant and inexorable. The first raindrops and a few hailstones began to hit me in the face.

I had to veer off-course to get onto the road by Frensham Great Pond and that sudden turn saved me from drowning. The storm's track had an astonishingly clear-cut outer limit and to my great surprise, I simply cycled across it into the dry. Like a blind, destructive dragon, the storm raged past,

flooding roads, smashing crops, knocking out power lines. I let it roll on for a bit, then continued more leisurely on my way, eventually catching up with some tremendous puddles. When I arrived at my cottage the Gaffer greeted me, saw that I was dry and unscathed and said, 'You missed a fantastic storm!'

CHAPTER SEVENTEEN

Hallucinatory Water

The sound level is going down. After about half an hour the drumming on the brolly (which has somehow withstood the cataract) is less deafening and the storm is subsiding. A well-rinsed treeline reappears in the distance and there is a luminous glow from the sky. The rain descends more gently and begins to sparkle, while a crack in the cloud opens wider and admits, suddenly, a melodramatic shaft of light, like something out of the Old Testament. It must be the finger of Isaak Walton guiding lost anglers towards their desire. The rain is merely sprinkling rather than thrashing the surface and the rings from each droplet are widening, separating, becoming less frequent. Yet more hypnotic.

Careful! As I stared, my tired eyes saw those rain rings metamorphose into the scales of a monster that stretched from bank to bank. It was only a momentary switch of focus, but it shows how the interior images are getting frustrated and how close they are to the surface. It's always interesting to starve yourself of sleep so utterly that you break the barrier between the exterior and interior worlds. It's a fact of our nature that if, for a long period, we don't dream - whether we remember our dreams or not - we can suffer psychological damage and even die. Therefore, if we hold back sleep long enough, yet remain passive, our dreams eventually clamour to be realised, and the world becomes infinitely more intriguing. I remember one evening after fifty hours without sleep, seeing a willow tree turn into a quite convincing cathedral and on a similar occasion, a duck spoke to me intelligibly. There was also a pond that unfolded at my feet and became a restaurant full of old friends.

When I was younger and even more obsessed I invariably became so immersed in the fishing that I'd ignore tiredness, hunger and exhaustion altogether. I'd fight off sleep until I reached a point when I'd almost forget what I was meant to be doing. And suddenly I would be doing something completely different from fishing, like crawling through the roof beams of some labyrinthine building or being pursued by dragons. Ultimately, sleep would catch up with me somewhere daft, like at the top of a lookout tree or in a patch of nettles, where I was stalking a big carp. I once fell asleep at Redmire and yet somehow remained alert and actively fishing. I dropped off at sunset, as I was leaning back against a tree, holding the rod and woke up in pitch darkness to find myself knee-deep in water, with the rod bending into a twenty five pound common carp.

The most exhausting, mind-draining exercise of all is to fish intently through a night while facing a stiff unrelenting wind. Trial by gale can destroy even the most resolute, enthusiastic or bone-headed angler. Nick and I once staggered away from a lake after such a test of endurance -

fishing for twenty hours, from noon till morning, into a minor hurricane. We both looked on the point of death - transparently pale - and we rode home on Nick's A.J.S., weaving through early-morning traffic as if the bike had contracted mad cow disease. I still don't understand how we made it. We reached home at about 9 a.m., slid off the saddle and left the bike on its side in the front garden with the rods and tackle strewn all round it. Somehow we managed to crawl upstairs to our respective beds where the flat plain of sheets awaited us like the divine centre of creation. After pulling the covers over my head, I purposefully held onto consciousness, wondering how long it would take before I fell into another dimension. I managed to last about ten seconds. We woke at midnight, made a tremendous feast and drank two bottles of wine. At 3 a.m. we returned to bed and slept solidly until noon when we picked up the pieces in the front garden and went fishing again.

The rain is just pricking the surface here and there. Only the branches continue to drizzle. The lake gleams brilliantly, even though the sun is again hidden in cloud. All the millions of tiny suspended fragments in the surface film have been sunk by the storm, leaving an immaculate sheen. The blue has spread across from east to west and soon the cloud will lift completely. And although the temperature has fallen a few degrees I remain confident of finding some feeding fish. Though there are no signs here yet, I think I'll go for a damp stroll along the bank, up towards the place where Isaak's finger was pointing.

Walking under the tall, dripping trees (there was a sweet scent of steaming leaf mould) I came suddenly on a line of enormous stone obelisks that loomed up as strangely as a mirage from the water's edge. But they were real enough; so was the heron that I startled, so was the galaxy of bubbles round the edge of a large lily bed and also the carp - only a small one, though - that turned almost silently on the surface. I leaned against the first obelisk, watching the water and within minutes the sun came dazzlingly out, obscuring all the details. I'd seen enough though. The depth was only about three feet round the lilies and most of the area on my side of them was thick with clouds of carp-stir. Isaak had not misled me.

I hurried back for my rod, slipped the float back on the line, baited with corn and flicked the tackle as close to the pads as possible. Scattering a few handfuls of groundbait, I sat back on a bit of wet stonework and awaited the results. Another carp rolled after a few minutes, much larger than the first one, and the wheeling ripple actually knocked my quill over. I tightened the line to tweak the float upright again, but it drew away from me.

Before I could react the rod lurched over and I found myself connected to a carp. It surged off making a ridge in the surface. Then it shot across in front of me, heading away from the lilies into open water. I didn't have to resort to any crude hauling and just coaxed it steadily towards the net. It was on the bank in a few moments, a pretty, sparkling common carp of about five pounds. I slipped him straight back, remembering the time when I bought my first carp rod and would have travelled a hundred miles for a fish of his size.

Bubbles still fizzed around the lilies and I cast again, and again, and again, each time having to wait only a few minutes before the float slid away and another portly, brilliantly gold carp came swirling gamely into the net. Though only one of them - a fish of about seven pounds - was big enough to steal more than a yard of line, I confess to being delighted about catching them. It was as if the lake had decided that, though I did not yet deserve anything sensational, it could offer me a few examples of its lesser treasures.

The sun became quite hot and most of the dampness steamed out of my jacket and the wall I was sitting on. I pulled my hat brim down so that my eyes were shaded and

I could see more clearly across the lake. Everything looked radiant and vivid, but almost too bright after the previous grey hours. I didn't bother to recast as it looked as if the carp had moved off and, anyway, I'd now qualified for my doze.

Leaning back against the stonework, I made myself comfortable and slipped quickly towards that sublime moment I'd been guarding against, when the conscious mind loses its hold. Though my eyes were shut and shaded by my hat I could still half-see the reflected sun. The surface wobbled and broke and the light pulsed against my closed eyelids. What was it? I wondered, but didn't look to see. Carp? Swan? Mermaid?

Beside the throbbing, slightly irritating light, there was also a sustained mental image which persisted right up to the moment when I drifted off. I felt like a willow going loose in a breeze or a stone sinking into a honey pot, yet I was still staring into a curiously unfading interior lake. It differed from the exterior one as it had an even more mysterious and seductive glow. Furthermore, as my mind darkened round the edges, so the lake brightened in contrast until it was almost on fire. I wasn't sure whether it was a premature dream or simply a reflexive after-image, the culmination of twenty slow hours beside shifting, lapping, hallucinatory water.

CHAPTER EIGHTEEN

The Art of Stalking

Judging by the position of the sun when I woke, I don't think I slept longer than an hour, not quite long enough to refresh the mind and restore the spirit. Actually, I felt worse than before, when I was merely tired. It seemed my head had become clay and my bones had turned into twisted metal. I suppose it must have been tea time when I opened my eyes.

Tea!, I thought, feeling suddenly better, but as I was about to sit up I sensed I was being watched. Instead of moving the whole of me, I merely moved a finger, pushing up the brim of my hat and peering surreptitiously along the bank.

There was no-one there, but a glance lakewards told me I was in the presence of one of the gods. Not ten yards out was the dark, cloudy form of quite a large carp. It wasn't actually looking at me, in fact, as it was browsing over the lake bed, sending up little puffs of silt, it was probably oblivious of me, but it was close enough to notice me if I moved. Three other carp were feeding alongside it, but they were much smaller, about the size of the ones I'd caught earlier. The big fish, however, was well into the twenties.

Waiting until he turned right away from me, I slid sideways to reach my rod, carefully removed the float and shot, baited the hook with corn and gently cast a yard in front of him.

He nosed down again and another mud cloud gradually blossomed around him, almost obscuring him. Then he pushed forward and hung motionless for a while in midwater. Because of the sun's angle I couldn't see clearly, even though he was so close; I could just discern the soft grey colour of his back and the pattern of his scales. The tail and fins hung almost limply. Abruptly, but for no apparent reason, he snapped out of his reverie and finned away towards the lilies, turning in a wide, slow half circle before sinking down to feed again about twenty yards away.

Watching him, I'd forgotten about the others, but I suddenly noticed my line twitching and instinctively struck. Fortunately, I failed to connect and one of the three small fish shot away round the lily bed. The others hovered nervously for a while, then slowly moved off, but the larger carp continued to feed.

I couldn't quite reach him without adding a single shot to the line and though the bait landed perfectly just beyond him, the little plop of the shot was just enough to disturb him and push him further away to my left, under the first of the overhanging trees. He didn't seem unduly ruffled and began to root around again. But I was in a bit of a quandary. Once you have disturbed a carp, however mildly, it is usually fatal to pursue it further. If it settles down again, though, and you can be patient, then eventually it will forget you and you can try another ruse. Of course, the trick is not to get the King in check until you are sure of your endgame - but then how can you be sure of anything when the grand master keeps changing the rules?

I reeled slowly in, put down the rod and crawled along the bank until I was in shadow - all my tiredness and stiffness suddenly forgotten. Rising to my feet I peered out over the water and watched the fish as it sifted through the silt. It was head down at an angle of about forty five degrees and as it truffled the tail gently wafted an inch or two below the surface, forming slow whorls. From my new, shaded viewpoint, I observed him in much greater detail and appreciated more fully the impressive dimensions. Like the big carp of yesterday, this one was very broad across the back yet did not possess any great depth. The width was remarkable though, right along to the wrist of the tail. The tail was almost fan-like but, oddly, the fins seemed disproportionally small, making the fish appear longer than it actually was.

No angler had ever hooked that carp or probably even cast for it before. Maybe no-one had even seen it before. It was unknown and enigmatic, right down to its vital statistics, its age and the provenance of its ancestors. It pushed forward again, just a few yards, trailing a pale cloud of mud, then began to browse once more, delicately sifting the lake bed for microscopic larvae, like a whale filtering plankton.

I tossed out a few dozen grains of corn, scattering them where I judged his next move would take him. Typically, he went in the opposite direction, heading directly out into the lake where he was joined suddenly by five companions. They simply materialised around him like a magical escort, each one almost his size. It seemed they'd decided to go right across the

119

lake, but after a few purposeful tail strokes they all became bored with the idea. The formation broke up about thirty yards out and they curved in separate directions, slowing to stillness.

They remain there now, even though I've been back to my original pitch to collect some more bait and this pen and notebook (that I'd deliberately left behind before). I have catapulted some little cat biscuits ten yards to their right, hoping the slight drift will bring the morsels directly over their heads. However, they'll probably ignore them. With aristocratic diffidence they float motionless just below the surface, meditating on their liquid sky.

I shall wait here in the shadows and see what happens. They look so obvious, so catchable, and yet they are at their most withdrawn and elusive. They are in a state of trance, but are not asleep, for just the shadow of a passing bird would have them instantly plunging into the depths, as would a careless footfall or even a shout. Maybe their eyes are now unseeing, but they can sense the whole world through their skins, reading vibrations and shadows and scents. Uncannily they can also detect the minute electro-discharges that pulse continually through the water. No radar is as sophisticated or as versatile.

In younger days I frequently drove myself mad casting for carp that looked as easy to catch as a sleeping kitten and yet were completely indifferent to my careful presentation and my sweet baits. Only if they woke unstartled from their aquadoze did they become more than merely tantalising, although however deep-seeming their slumber, however craftily I stalked them, when they finally stirred they invariably showed they'd been aware of me all along.

I remember, at a pond in Suffolk, taking great care climbing up an overhanging oak bough so that I could lower a bait precisely and delicately onto the nose of an enormous carp. It was lying in dappled shade a few inches below the surface, its

fins barely moving and only the quiet pulsing of the gills giving evidence of life. It would weigh probably thirty six or thirty seven pounds which, at the time, was the biggest carp I'd ever seen outside Redmire.

Having inched into position, I switched off the check on my centre-pin and slowly lowered a little piece of brown breadcrust down onto the water. I let it settle four feet in front of the fish and, as soon as it was waterlogged, eased it out with the rod tip directly over the carp's head. There was a slight breeze wafting across the pond and it drifted my bait across the fish's shoulders and washed it towards the bank. I teased it back gently in front of the fish again and so repeated my offer several times until the bread finally washed completely off the hook. Throughout, the carp never once moved, nor showed the slightest interest in the bait.

The texture of the bark began making a painful impression on me, even though I was wearing a thick pullover. So I shifted my weight and accidentally dislodged a bit of dead twig. It was only tiny and it landed with a minuscule plop several feet behind the fish, and yet it was as if someone had pressed a starter button. Immediately the gills began to work more powerfully, the dorsal rose up, the pectorals began to flap and the tail began to gently churn. However, the carp remained more-or-less stationary, like a ship at anchor stoking up its engines.

I was just wondering whether to rebait when the fish reversed, turned round and swam towards the bank. I guessed what was going to happen. The bit of sloppy bread had almost drifted into the roots under the bank and the carp cruised straight up to it and gulped it unhesitatingly down with a sharp 'cloop' that could have been heard half a mile away. Turning rather clumsily it surged off making a great bank-slapping wave, passed beneath me and headed out into the open lake. Of course I never saw it again.

The six grey backs are still clearly visible, looking like basking seals as they soak up the late afternoon sun. Not one has broken rank.

Once, as I stalked round a large Surrey lake, I noticed that same subtle but distinctive smokey grey showing vaguely in a narrow gap between lily pads. It looked no more obvious than a tea-stain on a cluttered tablecloth, but then the leaves parted and a big back momentarily appeared. It belonged to a carp of at least twenty pounds and almost before it had sunk slowly down again I cast a piece of crust several yards beyond it. Then I tweaked the bait back over the pads until it slid into the little strip of open water above the fish. Perhaps an hour passed, but the pale grey form did not stir again.

Eventually another, smaller carp appeared, a fish of about fifteen pounds, cruising round the edge of the lily bed to my left. It sniffed the surface, looking altogether a more temptable specimen, and so, after a moment's hesitation, I snicked the hook out of the crust and reeled in. But before I'd even had time to rebait and cast to the newcomer, there was a loud gurgle and the bread between the pads disappeared into a cavernous mouth. I didn't get a second chance.

Now and again, however, Isaak smiled on me. There was a little woodland pool I used to fish inhabited by a colony of carp so well-educated in the wiles of anglers that each one deserved a diploma in evasion and escapology. I knew fishermen who'd spent years trying unsuccessfully to outwit them. My method there was to quietly creep round the banks with my rod already made up and the hook baited. Usually I'd find a fish somewhere, but if I completed a circuit without seeing anything then I would either sit down and wait for a carp to appear or simply go home.

One warm July evening I arrived at the pool to find it deserted of anglers but also seemingly devoid of life. However when I was halfway round it, I noticed three static shapes poised beneath the surface in the pool's centre. I crouched down and waited and within a few minutes they began to swim very slowly towards my bank. The smallest was about fourteen pounds and the largest looked about twenty.

The Secret Carp

Pausing until I was certain they were on a fixed course, I cast well in front of them, with four cat biscuits on a size 8. The carp swam in a line, the biggest in the lead. He saw the bait and came directly up to it, but only sniffed it; then continued on his way. Yet before the second carp arrived, he went round in a quickening circle and rose again, taking the bait without any fuss, leaving just a thin circle of ripple spreading across the surface. There was a violent downswirl when I struck and the fish headed for the lilies on the far bank. I was only using five pound line, but it was perfectly balanced with a slow-action Mark Four Avon and I was able to ease the carp to a stop within twenty five yards.

After that it was simply a series of deep plunges and circlings before it finally rolled splashily under the rod tip. When it saw the net it made another long lunge, but again I brought it to a halt before the danger zone. After a spell of tail lashing, it wallowed round and sailed back over the net before realising quite where it was going.

Quickly, I hoisted the mesh up and the fish spun round like a catherine wheel and nearly broke the frame. When it had quietened, I carefully unhooked and weighed it. Nineteen pounds, six ounces - a mirror carp and, despite my slight prejudice against mirrors, a splendid-looking fish, his flanks the colour of an autumn oak and his back as smooth and purple as a Victoria plum.

There is a tendency among carp anglers nowadays to fish predominantly at long range and while it is obvious that a carp a hundred yards away won't be aware of the angler, it is also true that, for most of the time, the angler won't be aware of the carp. On a crowded lake this might be an advantage, but I find that the further I get away from my quarry the less exciting he becomes. For me, the ultimate angling experience is to get so close to a large carp that I can almost touch it. It can give you quite a shock to realise that you can't actually cast: first because you're almost paralysed by the proximity, and secondly because your rod tip has reached beyond the fish. If it's a real colossus, especially if it's one you have spent months or even years dreaming about, the sudden confrontation can crack your teeth.

This is surely the essence of carp angling; the concrete reality after the previous half-imagined glimpses; the monster so close that the rest of the world dissolves around it. Your heart can sound like an engine with a blown gasket, particularly if, after creeping forward, you can lower a bait in front of it and watch the monster's reactions. These occasional moments of high drama are unknown to the angler who habitually fishes at long range. He will also be denying himself useful observations, for only when you are really close to a carp can you appreciate how delicately and fastidiously it uses its large prehensile lips, how it picks and sifts, funnels and blows, how it avoids tackle and inspects bait while effortlessly balancing and shifting its body weight with its fins and tail. And finally, if it does pick up the bait, and you connect, you will never be so severely tested. At long range, because a carp's power is absorbed by the elasticity of the line, even the most energetic fish can feel sullen. At close range the encounter can be overwhelming.

The best approach, of course, is to mix methods, but I shall always prefer stalking because, apart from its more dramatic aspects, it is such a simple and effective form of angling. I hate cluttering myself up and always carry the absolute minimum of tackle and bait - just the rod and net in my hands and the rest either in my pockets, or in a small creel or shoulder bag. That's all you need to catch the biggest fish that swims.

CHAPTER NINETEEN

The View from the Depths

The sun has just begun to lose its intensity, though the sky seems clearer than it was this morning. It is that moment, that change of phase between afternoon and evening, when everything pauses before the slow descent towards night. The big fish are still out there. While I've been writing, they have been basking or dreaming or conspiring or whatever it is they like doing. I've baited with two red worms and cast out near but not amongst them. From time to time I've flicked a free cat biscuit or a bit of crust over them, but they have ignored everything.

I get the feeling that they are conscious of my presence but they know I pose no threat. I'm like a hunter without an arrow or a burglar confounded by a baffling lock. They are, I'm certain, uncatchable, at least for the moment. While it's likely that, when they finally rouse themselves, they'll simply steam off towards the far horizon, they may instead just spread out and begin feeding, in which case there is hope for me. I shall sit here, waiting, and see what happens.

A dabchick swims past, spots me, but doesn't dive. The faintest breeze flows round me but barely quivers a leaf. As the sun has moved round into the north-west I can see the carp better, but because they've hardly moved all this time their appearance seems to have altered. They now look less like fish and more like chunks of masonry, like the broken columns of some drowned archaic monument. The obelisks next to me are the only remnants left intact.

Many years ago I found another lake a bit like this one, but where the surroundings were even more like an ancient ruin. Or perhaps I should say it was even more like an abandoned theatre, with all the old sets - the follies, the statues and monuments - left standing in odd places. I didn't catch any monster carp, in fact I didn't even cast, but I did have an unforgettable night there.

It was in 1969, when Nick, Jasper and I were at the height of our lake hunting days. We had marked down a blue dot on our map for that day's exploration and after a ride to the Surrey-Sussex border, we left our bikes on the edge of a vast heath and set off on foot towards a distant wood. Halfway through the trees we came up against a high ivy-clad wall which ran along the edge of a valley.

We crossed the wall and there below us lay a large irregular-shaped lake. The banks were wooded, there were statues and baroque style follies standing around the water's edge, there were overgrown islands and also a kind of dwarf Matelot tower poking up out of a bay. Three anglers were fishing from this tower and we presumed, because we couldn't see any boat, they'd either been ferried out there or they had a boat moored out of sight. From the colour and from the general appearance of the place, we were convinced we were looking at a carp lake and immediately marked it down on the list of future prospects. Then we saw the three anglers descend into the tower and Nick suddenly said, 'They're going to reappear on the bank!' Jasper and I shook our heads, yet after a couple of minutes they popped up at the water's edge like rabbits out of a hat. They proceeded across a wide lawn and disappeared behind a clump of trees.

We all smiled, gazing down at the tower, our eyebrows maintaining a fairly high altitude. This lake was more than merely carpish and picturesque, it was also wonderfully eccentric. However, there was no doubt that it was seriously private and well-keepered and therefore a casual daylight inspection was clearly ill advised. But the moon was almost full and we vowed to return after the pubs had closed.

It was a good day for discoveries because we went off and found that the local pub just happened to be the oldest in the county, with the atmosphere to match. Quiet, cloistered and dark, it was the ideal place to prepare for one of life's great adventures.

At about midnight we crossed the wall again and picked our way through dappled moonlight under the trees and down to the lake. We came onto a track that ran along the western bank and followed it round to a little ornamental bridge that took us across an inlet stream and onto the north bank. There we hesitated and listened. The night was not quite silent for there was an intermittent breeze threading through the trees, linking the intervals of perfect stillness. The lake looked like a table of black velvet with a lamp in the middle of it that was the reflected moon. When the breeze blew the lamp seemed to smash into a million pieces. Lending an added touch of whimsy was the statue of Neptune rising out of the water between us and the distant tower. In the brittle light it looked almost as if he'd come to life.

We could see no lit windows of lodge or manor, though we knew from the map that we were close to such buildings. Quietly we continued along the water's edge, convinced that if we found the entrance to a tunnel we would also find a locked door. We came upon what looked like a gigantic, elaborately ornamented manhole cover. Spiralling down to one side of it was a flight of steps which led us into total blackness. Naturally, we didn't have a torch. Only amateurs carried torches. We had to feel our way down with our feet and were eventually stopped in our tracks by the anticipated door. I turned the heavy iron handle and pulled but it didn't budge. So I heaved and it gave suddenly, flying open and slamming back against a stone wall with an unbelievable reverberating crash. We all fled back up the steps, emerging into brilliant moonlight, thinking that every keeper and his dog within miles would be bearing down on us. But there was only the faint hiss of the breeze and after a few minutes, with no hint of any menacing sounds, we returned to the open doorway, stepping ever so lightly through it and feeling our way forward by spreading our arms wide and running our fingers along the smooth walls of a passage.

We had gone only a dozen or so yards when we stopped short at the sight of a weird green glow emanating from another doorway. It couldn't, we realised, be a door to the tower because we had not come far enough under the lake. Perhaps it was a secret room and the light was on because someone was there, waiting for us. However, hearing no sounds other than our own breathing and convincing ourselves there was no danger, we shuffled cautiously on, approaching not a doorway but a place where the passage opened into an unbelievable glass dome. We staggered into it and gazed up through the depths at a green, aqueous moon.

It was like Captain Nemo's dream, or perhaps Noah's nightmare: an observation room at the bottom of a lake. It was not constructed solely of glass but consisted of solid glass blocks set into a cleverly engineered stone framework, like a glass-lined lobster pot. And while much of the lower exterior was cloudy with algae the upper half was mostly clear, yet not, because of the width of the glass, perfectly transparent. When the breeze rippled the surface we saw, opaquely, the moon looking as if it had been spread over us like butter.

After we had recovered enough to continue, we groped down the rest of the passage, stumbling onto another flight of steps that led us up into the tower and eventually out into the open air.

Sitting more or less where the anglers had been fishing, we looked out across the lake and wondered what kind of genius had created it. Even Capability Brown hadn't struck on the idea of continuing his designs underwater. And if there was this sub-surface dome maybe there were other such miracles hidden elsewhere below the lake.

Then we decided that the lake could not have been designed by man; it was obviously the work of an enterprising fish. While men kept little fish in bowls full of water this fish kept men in bowls full of air and spent his years studying their curious behaviour.

131

The breeze came again and the crest of a great silver-edged cloud appeared over the trees. We agreed it was time to head home. Pausing once more inside the luminous dome, we had a last view through the depths. A shadow went across the moon. Nick said it was the cloud, Jasper said it was a pirate ship, but I said it was the lake's creator, swimming down to view his new specimens.

CHAPTER TWENTY

Another Kind of Life

Over the last half-hour the carp have all dispersed in several different directions. Two of them - though not the largest pair - began to probe about near my bait, sending up clouds of bubbles, and there was a tense moment when I saw the line jag and tighten. Yet just as I was going to strike, it fell slack. There was a mighty swirl and both carp streaked away like meteors. That was my chance and I missed it. A few bubbles are peppering the surface near the lilies but I suspect the area has been vacated by all but the smallest fish.

Now I really must have a cup of tea. In fact right now I need a cup of tea even more than I need a fish. I shall return to base camp and completely ignore any carp I might see on my way. Tea is of the essence ...

A cup of tea in the evening sunlight. Even if the long day had led only to this I couldn't complain. The perfect conclusion. But I still have hopes of another fish, especially now the light is changing. The trees on the west bank have become silhouettes and the lake has a more intense, more concentrated look about it. Just now I heard a big splash from along the far bank and I shall have to go and investigate as it may be that the carp are patrolling along the more shadowy margins. But I've made a full tea-pot and, naturally, I'm in no hurry ...

A non-angling friend said to me recently, 'It's a great mystery to me why you spend so much time fishing.' I asked him whether he'd ever been attracted to water when he was a child and he said no. He'd never felt particularly drawn to water because, firstly, there was no water near his childhood home and secondly, his parents believed that wet and mud were unnecessary evils: they would have forbidden him even to approach the sort of places where I spent all my formative years.

Maybe there is a kind of truth here. All those people who find it so hard to understand anglers are surely people who have had a deprived childhood. They might have been penniless orphans in a concrete desert or they might have had wealthy parents, lived in a mansion and had the best education money could buy. But they never learnt the most important lesson of all: water is a child's best friend. Water is magical. It behaves in a manner totally different from anything else in the dry world. It is also a stimulant and an hallucinogen: simply by staring at it a child can dissolve in it. It can reflect strange moods. It can be cheerful, but also terrifying, especially where the river or pond bed shelves down into sudden depths. It is a universe for another kind of life.

Just watch a child's expression as he or she marvels at a newt or a stickleback or a tadpole in its own environment. The eyes flex in wonder and no television or cinema or theme park could inspire quite that intensity of emotion. But watch again when the child sees a big resplendent fish ghosting by. The wonder changes to incredulity, fear, awe and then, invariably, laughter. That such a creature could exist in this cosy familiar world! I've seen that expression many times, first in my childhood friends and now in my own children; an open-mouthed shock of surprise and delight, as if the revelation confirmed everything they suspected about the magic and power of water.

Of course a child may never think of water as anything more than wonderful stuff to play with. He may be completely indifferent to the strange life within it and concerned only with throwing stones, launching toy boats or building dams. He at least recognises the fundamental attraction of water even though he may never know about monsters, as he will always be looking in the wrong direction.

A child may also become blasé, especially if he or she accompanies father on successful angling jaunts and becomes accustomed to seeing nets full of large fish. Before her first birthday, my daughter, Camilla, was stroking the fins of carp, barbel, salmon and pike all bigger than her, and now she is seven the depths of lakes and rivers hold few mysteries for her. She does, however, swim like a fish. I am more concerned about my four year old son, Alexander. Last summer he caught more carp than me. It's true they were mostly under a pound in weight, but most of them were 'tickled' out of the village pond by hand. I suppose I should really be proud of him. Yet whether life below the surface eventually becomes merely fascinating to my children, whether they become anglers or not, they will, at least, always understand an angler's motivation. And of course they will never lose their love of water or their ability to dream themselves into it.

I have often encountered another species of child who is actually repelled by water and who fails to respond to anything but the artificial material world. These unfortunate creatures cannot appreciate nature in any form and, even more unfortunately, there are a lot of them about. They treat life like a computer game with nothing but a blank screen between rounds. Quite often, they grow up to become interested in power and politics and because they will never understand anglers, they represent a dangerous threat.

Yet, thinking back to my sceptical friend's words, how many anglers really stop and think objectively about angling? Stand back and it is, superficially, an extremely irrational occupation, especially if you are repeatedly catching the same kind of fish and putting them back. To someone with no understanding of anglers, it must appear lunatic. To spend so much time trying to catch an alien-looking creature which is then immediately released; to spend so much money on tackle and bait and licences; to form so many little clubs and societies, each with conflicting attitudes and opinions regarding exactly the same basic exercise. Surely the entire modern angling world is one enormous, extravagant fantasy?

To my puzzled non-angling friend I said that fishing is like a game of chess against an unpredictable opponent, with long contemplative pauses between moves.

'So it's a kind of challenge, eh?' he said.

No, not really a challenge. Nor really a competition - or at least not in the way I see it. So my allusion to chess is confusing. I had to agree that match fishing was probably the most indefensible form of angling because the individual fish meant nothing more than points in a system of scoring, and the fishing itself, however skilled, was nothing more than a race. Match fishing is certainly a sport and yet because we associate that word with competitiveness, point-scoring and attainment. But I can't define *my* fishing as a sport. Nor is it a hobby or pastime.

'So how *would* you define it?' asked my friend.

I told him it was simply a different kind of life. It's not, to me, anything special - it is normal and everyday. The wet world it inhabits has, down the years, flooded naturally over the dry world and now I'm always conscious of it whether I'm on the bank or not. Rivers and lakes constantly swill about in my head, fantastic fish leap out of the most mundane thought. I am obsessive, incurable. I have become amphibious. There are, of

course, decisive moments, otherwise everything would just sink into an agreeable haze. My fishing is adventurous as well as reflective and there are places like this lake which give it a real sense of drama. Drama, in fact, is an essential element, stemming directly from my childhood experiences. Once I had learnt that monsters haunted my own village pond I could never again look at a stretch of water without sensing the dramatic potential which is the inspiration for all anglers. The discovery elevated even the tiniest pools onto a level beyond the ken of ordinary mortals, despite the fact that some of the places I fished held nothing but leeches and snails. Nowadays, it takes a water like the one I am sitting beside to incite me and inspire that same sense of impending drama.

'And do you come home long-faced if you don't catch anything?'

No, of course not. There are always memorable qualities about even the most fishless day. Only those anglers who demand constant action ever have blank days. Yet there's no denying the extra glow in the evening if, after a long day, you land a good fish. And if it's a really good fish then you come home singing like a drunk at an opera. Alternatively, if you fall into the 'straight rod syndrome' - many days passing without the slightest sign of a fish - then you can become troubled and less able to appreciate your surroundings. To begin with it doesn't matter, but then you start thinking that you've lost your touch and the more the fish avoid you the more prone you are to tangles, miscasts and attacks by swans, mosquitos and Apaches. Yet none of this is as bad as hooking and losing a great fish and the worst thing in the world is to lose your fishing altogether, as a result of pollution or abstraction or disease or drought or - perhaps not so destructive, but equally pernicious - because of poachers or rich syndicates.

'To get back to your original question,' I said, 'about how much time I spend fishing. The truth is that I don't spend nearly as much time fishing as I used to, now I have discovered that my paternal instinct is just as strong as my angling instinct.'

One of my earliest rules was *never compromise*, but now I break that rule constantly as I become more and more absorbed in my own children. But if I have less time for the waterside it has ensured that I now savour my time there even more completely. I like to think it has also made me a more efficient angler, for if I've left the cottage at teatime and promised to be back to tell a bedtime story then I've only got an hour or so to catch a fish. And the less time I have, the more positive I must be before making that crucial cast. I may only have one chance per outing, but I make more of my chances nowadays (usually!). Long days like these are even more priceless than they were when I was living like a gipsy. On other days the fishing is more active but more relaxed as I rediscover the magic of tiddler-snatching through my childrens' eyes.

Watching their reaction to a minnow in a jam jar is like looking at a very bad artist who has just completed a masterpiece. The tiddler is like their own creation, but they can hardly believe it. They want to see it even more closely and lovingly. They want to touch it, to keep it for ever, even though they know by experience that it would lose its iridescence and its vibrancy if it died. It is this conjuring up of a miracle that makes fishing so fascinating to them. The benefit is that it brings them closer to nature and by appreciating nature they will ultimately appreciate the world and their place in it.

'And do you feel the same towards a big fish now,' asked my persistent friend, 'as you did towards tiddlers when you were young?'

'More or less,' I said.

'Right then,' he said, with the tone of a psychiatrist who has been taking notes. 'To sum up: you are an angler because you spent your childhood splashing about in water and just happened to notice a large fish. Your discovery altered your world view and caused your interest in fish to be raised to the level of worship. Fishing is now like a religion and you have recently initiated your children into its arcane rituals. On the other hand, you are a fisherman because you have never grown up!'

I liked his arguments, but I had to point out that we had not even mentioned the most important, primary ingredient in the making of an angler: the fishing gene, the ancestral spark that is brighter in some than in others and lies dormant in the blood of the majority. Whatever the circumstances, that gene will sometimes insist that a person becomes an angler. Denying it expression is like denying that person air.

'So you're behaving like a child *and* a caveman!' he said.

CHAPTER TWENTY ONE

A New Rod

All day I have been on the east bank but now I am fishing a small overgrown island that stands just out from the west bank. It is a bit like the hub of a cartwheel with various fallen trees radiating outwards like spokes. One of those trees reaches the main bank so I didn't have to wade out here. In the open water between two sun-bleached tree trunks, my float looks pert and expectant. Clutches of bubbles are rising all around it.

Perhaps half an hour ago, after my second cup of tea, I went and stood on the dam, looking for signs; and though nothing stirred in the deep shadow under the trees, I felt drawn to this spot and now suspect that my hunch is about to pay off. It is about an hour before sunset. The lake sways to that same slow, immense rhythm that I noticed at dawn. Moreover, as I'm in shadow again, facing a brilliantly lit treeline, it is now like a re-creation of that hour after sunrise. Except that the light is steadily diminishing and if I wait here long enough I'll see the moon coming up in the −

141

My heart valves have just been shivered by my float. It flicked as if a bee had flown into it and then slid an inch to the left. If it moves again ...

I have a carp here just like the old threepenny bit; the same colour, the same shape and not much bigger. It is exquisite. It must weigh about a pound - deep-bodied, high-backed and its scales absolutely scintillating. He flickers away into the depths and I'll cast again for his great grandfather.

Surprising how damp it is here. The sun hasn't penetrated along this bank since the cloudburst and the grass and vegetation are still sparkling with moisture. Another bite, but nothing develops. Bubbles still starring the surface. Bait was stolen when I reeled in.

Since I had the idea of packing all this minutiae into a notebook (all of it in my own inimitable shorthand) I was obviously hoping to record the capture of a glorious specimen, but having watched the reaction of those fish by the obelisks I now feel less confident. The carp I lost this morning was one of those almost-very-lucky flukes (that I'm so good at cultivating). I presumed at the time that it at least proved the effectiveness of sweetcorn, but despite ideal conditions, I have only managed one decent wildie, four gold bottles and a threepenny bit. Yet it's been a splendid day.

Another reason I wanted a magnum-sized carp was that I wanted to write a letter to the maker of my rod, Edward Barder, telling him how it had stood the test. This is the prototype of the *Bishop* (named after my fifty-one pounder), a lovely length of hand-crafted split cane that Edward is eventually going to market. Two piece, eleven feet, it is just a curve more versatile than the standard cane *Mark Four* and altogether much swisher and more pleasant to use. Edward, who used to work for Hardy's but is now a full-time free-lance cane splitter, has built me three rods now, two for carp and one for barbel. The latter, the *Barbus Maximus* has had the most use. Being a river rod it would anyway have had to work harder than the others as I like to keep a rod constantly in my hand when

I'm barbel or chub fishing. I christened it with a ten pound barbel and it has been teasing out wonderful fish ever since. I christened the *Bishop* with an eight pound wildie, then almost landed an enormous fish on it, but was outwitted at the last moment. That story is worth re-telling because it led directly to the newest Barder rod. It also gives me a perfect excuse to relive the sort of adventure I hoped would happen here. (I should add that my fondness of split cane is not just because I prefer my rods to be individually hand-made rather than mass-produced out of synthetic materials. Cane is actually superior for playing big fish than carbon fibre or any other type of rod).

I had kindly been given permission to spend a couple of days on a jewel of a pool in the Savernake Forest. It was one of those exclusive syndicate waters where you would never normally be privileged to fish unless one of the members died or you married the chairman's daughter. It was about the same size as Redmire, but lacked any great depth. Beautifully sheltered from the weather and the world, it nestled deeply in a wooded valley, surrounded by alders, willows and oaks. The carp grew quite large and fish of thirty pounds were a possibility.

Conditions were ideal when I got to the pool on my first day. It was a grey, misty dawn after a drizzly night and I found a group of feeding fish within minutes of my arrival. I quickly tackled up, using my new *Bishop*, a pre-war Altex No.2 loaded with twelve-pound line and a size six hook. Baiting with a natural jelly that neither I nor anyone else had ever tried for carp before, I cast, freeline, directly into a mass of bubbles and unfurling silt. It seemed a long wait, but eventually the line drew taut and I connected to a fish that chugged steadily and heavily up the pool. However, it had not travelled ten yards before the hook flicked out.

Resisting the temptation to chew a lump of flint, I tetchily re-cast and within half an hour was again bending into a large carp. The first one had felt large, but this one felt enormous. Again I lost it almost immediately, the throat teeth severing the ten pound braided trace (I had not experienced a 'bite off' for years!). The effect of this second loss was not unlike being struck in the face with a sack of frog spawn. Temporarily disabled, I went for a limp round the pool and was restored by the sight of a large slow ripple spreading out from beneath the branches of an ancient tree. After crawling through the brambles and nettles, I edged myself up the leaning, mossy trunk and peered down into the dark water.

There appeared to be a deep hollow in the lake bed but it was difficult to see clearly because of the shadow. The surface was being ruffled by some substantial carp and as I stared

A New Rod

I had a brief but glorious vision. The unseen creature suddenly flipped sideways and ran its flank momentarily across the lake bed. The gold curve looked like a sunken moon.

Holding my breath, I eased myself in reverse through the undergrowth and hurried back for rod, net and bait. Of course, with the over-hanging branches, the situation was inappropriate for an eleven-foot rod, but I hadn't brought my shorter stalking rod as its tip had recently been smashed (by a car door!). No matter. I wormed myself back to the oak, threading the rod and net alongside me and finally inched the rod-tip very gradually out from behind the trunk. Before lowering the bait into position, I tried to foresee what was going to happen if the carp snaffled it. Many of the branches swept down into the water and then reared up again from the depths and there was a complex interweaving of gnarled boughs that looked like a convention of congers. It was not the most inviting place I'd ever cast into, but certainly one of the most exciting.

I dropped the bait into the shadow and it sank slowly out of sight. Checking everything was in order, I leaned against the trunk, rod held ready. Within a minute the line cut smoothly through the surface and I struck firmly. There was a great uprush of water, then a big wave that shot straight between the sunken branches and out into open water. In the split second before it fled, I had a clear sight of a mirror carp that was at least thirty pounds.

I pushed the rod tip under water and jumped in, sinking deep in soft silt. Despite the tight clutch, the twelve pound line was streaming off the spool and it continued to stream, with my finger getting hot on the rim, as I heaved myself forward and then pulled myself up with my free hand onto a submerged bough. Playing a big carp while balancing precariously on a slippery branch is not recommended. You suddenly realise how important it is to maintain a firm foothold, to be able to shift your weight to counteract the pull and the changes of direction. The carp was heading for the trees on the far bank, eighty yards away, and it almost made them. I was amazed at its power.

Because of the pool's general shallow nature, the sweeps and turns were all the more spectacular and after five minutes the place looked like the haunt of a phantom speedboat. And with all of the branches over my head, I couldn't raise the rod high enough to exert its full strength. Nevertheless I did almost get the fish within range. It swam round in a big half-circle and I kept the pressure as firm as possible. It wallowed and rolled nearer, but then began coming in much too fast, heading ominously for the nest of snags. I slacked off and the carp rolled and headed away again, lunging to my right. But it picked up too much speed and by the time I'd applied the brakes it was too late. The line didn't snap but the hook was neatly transferred into the underside of another half-submerged tree fifty yards up the bank. I didn't see another fish for the rest of that day.

My next visit was not until some five weeks later. I'd described to Edward what had happened and said that if only I'd used a dwarf *Bishop* that carp would have been mine (how comforting it is to be able to blame one's tools).

'I'll make you a proper stalking rod,' he said.

'For big carp,' I said, 'and even bigger snags!'

We discussed specifications and it was designed,

made and delivered within a month - a superbly crafted, perfectly balanced, extremely powerful bit of stick. I had wanted to call it the *Curate* or the *Parson* but finally decided that ecclesiastic carp rods might offend the agnostics. So we called it the *Carpcrawler*.

'I actually tried to break it,' said Edward, 'by tying on some twenty pound line and nearly pulling my work bench over.' I winced and checked more closely to see if it was still straight. It was.

On my second trip I was not only allowed to fish throughout the night prior to the allotted day, I was even allowed a tea-making, net-wielding gillie. This invaluable person - my companion in rods, Shaun Alonso Linsley - thought this a terrific idea as he was also allowed to bring his own rod.

We got down at sunset and over a cup of tea watched the fish prickling the amber reflections with bubbles. When the bats appeared and the light began to fade we cast our baits along a relatively snag-free stretch of bank. But though fish were obviously moving past us in the dark water neither of us could attract their attention. All night the moon illuminated the valley, but then the silver glow became duller and the shadows less intense and, almost before we realised it, dawn had quietly arrived. When the light was strong enough I crept round to the oak cave, but it was uninhabited. Nor was there any evidence of fish elsewhere. As the new day had advanced so the carp had withdrawn.

Then the sun rose and I proudly tackled up with the new rod. It still smelt of fresh varnish. After coupling it with a *Swallow* centrepin and twelve pound line I tried a few speculative casts along the bank, working gradually back towards the oak cave. Though no one had been at home earlier I guessed that, as the sun grew stronger, something might venture there for shade and sanctuary. Sure enough, as I peered round the tree immediately adjacent to the tangle of branches, I saw a slight furling on the surface just like that other time. A big tail was gently stirring the shadowed water and the faint disturbance actually began to shift towards me. Even under the cascade of overhanging branches it wasn't difficult to make an underhand Wallis cast, dropping the bait silently a yard in front of the riffle.

I crouched down and after a short pause the line between rod tip and surface suddenly fell slack, quivering as it did so. I wound and struck and a black hole spiralled open, revealing churned up leaf mould and a blaze of scales. I'd hooked a big carp that was pointing towards the bank and instead of turning it shot immediately forward and nearly struck a tree root. With a great tail swipe, it wheeled round and surged directly past me. The rod went into a superb bend and brought the fish straight to the surface, leading it in a wide, erratic circle before it dug down again with its pectorals. The centrepin was much more effective than a fixed spool reel because of the more direct control, allowing me to keep within ounces of the line's breaking strain.

As I shouted for the net there was a thunderous splash and the carp launched itself into open water. Again the rod came down with exactly the right amount of restraint and after a few reel-screeching seconds, the fish rolled heavily on the surface and was brought straight back under the trees. Typically, my gillie didn't hear me. Shaun was just then stalking a fish way up by the inlet stream, out of earshot. However, I was

148

in luck. The generous person who ran the syndicate had come down to see how we were faring and had also brought his own gear for a spot of fishing. I heard him call, then saw him crashing towards me through the undergrowth, net in hand.

'That's a good fish,' he gasped as he hustled in between the bankside branches and pushed the net out. The carp turned in a tight circle, but couldn't gather enough momentum to break out of it and eventually curved just within reach. I raised the rod a few inches higher, the net came up and in tumbled a terrific-looking fish. Gracefully shaped and vividly coloured, it was probably the most beautiful mirror carp I'd ever seen. The back was a deep mulberry and the peachy flanks were entirely covered with large, irregular overlapping scales. It weighed just over twenty one pounds.

'Thank you,' I said to the fish, the emergency gillie and the rodmaker.

CHAPTER TWENTY TWO

Harmonic Convergence

The puddles are ripening in the sunset as I sit here on the dam, taking in the last of the day. Looking up the length of the lake the curious jade tint to the water has gone and the entire surface smoulders like molten ore. Swallows and swifts swoop low overhead, mingling - just as they did at this time yesterday - with the first bats. Like torches about to be snuffed out the trees on the east bank still have their tops in sunlight, but everything else is in shadow. Apart from a few sideways jiggers of the float, there was no more activity on the island and the bubbles petered out within the hour. Furthermore, silver pirates began to leap about all over the place and I didn't want to have another argument with one of them.

I have a lot to learn about this place and probably the best way of discovering its secrets is not, as I suggested earlier, by constantly fishing, but simply by spending more time quietly wandering about and watching. Visiting it regularly, under different kinds of conditions, I might find out if the carp follow certain patterns of behaviour. Some kinds of routine become self-evident if you can observe fish over a long enough period. Though they will never become completely predictable, I might discover just enough to enable me to catch a few good ones.

After seven years of watching the Redmire carp, when I finally thought I understood the complex rules of that particular team, they would still come up with some baffling surprises. There will always be this element of mystery about carp, and even where the fishing is conducted like a scientific experiment, the carp will confound their observers, avoiding classification, like ghosts.

From watching the Redmire carp I learnt that certain groups of fish liked to follow a set routine while others lived a more individual, independent life. It was these nonconformists that I usually fished for. The groups of conventionalists were sometimes so fond of their habits that they would even bask in formation, lying in a particular pattern in the weedbeds. If the group broke up in the evening it could often be found in the same place the next day, each carp in precisely the same position as before. Waiting for one of these groups to 'switch on' and feed on your bait might take a week because the entire group would have to be persuaded rather than a single individual. I was never patient enough, nor organised enough to have more than a perfunctory cast towards one of these shoals. I preferred stalking the loners, especially as these solitary beings were often the largest in the pool.

Occasionally, one of the group-minded fish would behave uncharacteristically. One evening I was fishing the Redmire shallows, watching a group of about ten twenty-pounders drifting under the willows on the far bank. As they turned and began to head back down the pool, one of them broke ranks and swam directly towards me. I was float fishing a bunch of maggots and the carp came almost thirty yards in a straight line and went immediately down on the bait. Such was my amazement that I missed on the strike and the carp hurried back towards his companions, with the sort of expression that said, 'Why on earth did I do that?' Another smaller carp had been patrolling the centre of the shallows and as the larger one fled past so he turned and came back along the line of flight until he reached the bait. Like the bigger fish, he took it without hesitation and I duly landed a fifteen pound common.

On another day I drifted in the punt down the length of the pool and, without touching the paddles, merely let the faint movement of air waft me slowly along. As I floated towards a dense weed bed I could see a dozen or so big carp lying with their backs almost breaking the surface, but they all submerged on my arrival. A minute or two after I'd passed by they began to re-surface in the same positions, all except one, a big mirror carp, who began to follow in my wake. For nearly fifty yards it kept quite closely behind me until I came up gently against another even thicker weed bed and stopped drifting altogether. The fish disappeared beneath the punt.

There was another group of basking fish in this weed bed and I decided to try and tempt one by casting a big bunch of maggots onto the surface and twitching it back until it was right on a fish's nose. It took me perhaps ten minutes, but eventually I had a size 8 hook loaded with a dozen maggots, perfectly positioned inches above the head of a thirty pounder. Suddenly the gills began to puff and the fins began to fan as the fish woke up to the fact that breakfast had been miraculously served. It opened its huge lips and rose up, but at that exact moment there was an explosion to my left that was like a depth-charge going off. I turned to see the big mirror carp surging down the way he'd come and when I looked back to the weed bed all the other fish had vanished. Was that coincidence or had the mirror, being closest, suddenly realised what I was up to?

It was certainly no coincidence when, on another occasion, a big fish went down on a piece of macaroni only to be shouldered aside at the crucial moment by another, smaller carp who was definitely not competing for the bait. The larger fish turned, then moved again for the bait and was again, much to my despair, herded away by his bodyguard. The same kind of thing has happened elsewhere and I remember, at Waggoners' Wells in Hampshire, seeing a mirror carp of around fifteen pounds being shepherded away from my bait repeatedly by another fish of ten pounds. I was fishing a crust on the surface and the guardian finally began to barge its more witless counterpart away by pushing it amidships. But in doing so its tail cut across the surface and snagged my line. Instantly it bolted, but somehow remained tethered. It seemed terribly unfair on such a wise creature, but eventually I landed it and as it wallowed in the net, I couldn't resist saying, 'Serves you right!'

Other anglers have also noticed that certain carp within a colony are more intelligent than the others and will control the behaviour of their less circumspect or less experienced fellows. But there are times when they all seem under the control of another more mysterious influence, like when, for no apparent reason, and after hours of inactivity, two carp will leap simultaneously at different ends of the lake.

I once spent twenty-four hours fishing at Sheepwash with Jasper. We fished in adjacent pitches as we had only one landing net between us, but for about twenty hours neither of us had had even a twitch of interest from the carp. At

about noon I said to Jasper, 'I'm just going to sneak off up to the shallows. I'll shout for the net if I need it.'

'Funny you should say that,' said Jasper. 'I was just thinking of sneaking down to the dam. We'll leave the net here and you can pick it up as you dash to my assistance.'

'No,' I said, 'it'll be you who does the dashing.'

So we parted, each going to the opposite ends of the long pool. (I should add that I had been to look for fish on the shallows earlier, but there had been nothing to see).

Immediately on my arrival, I saw a carp moving in a weed bed and cast a crust to him. He took it almost nonchalantly, I struck and there was a wonderful boil in the water followed by a searing dive towards a reed bed. I let out a piercing whistle at precisely the same moment that Jasper's shout echoed across the water. 'Bring the net!' he yelled. It was a devilishly well-timed coincidence.

More peculiar than this was the coincidence concerning the number thirteen. In September 1973, I caught a nice carp at Redmire. Rod Hutchinson landed it for me and he immediately recognised it as a fish he'd grassed earlier that season. It was a very distinctive leather carp of over twenty seven pounds. Of course we compared our encounters and, in the course of our conversation, I said that the fish was my thirteenth carp over twenty pounds. Rod did a quick bit of accounting and said that, curiously, it had also been *his* thirteenth twenty-pounder. Then, five years later the same fish was caught again by Barry Mills. I was with him when he landed it and so told him about the coincidence. It got him thinking, he drew up a list and discovered the carp was also *his* thirteenth twenty-pounder. And this wasn't the end of the sequence for not long after I'd caught my fifty one and a half pounder Rod wrote to me from France to say that he'd just landed his best carp. *Fifty one and a half pounds!*

I hear that Barry is on the track of a big fish in the west country and, of course, I know exactly what it weighs. I'll no doubt hear from him soon. Unlike Rod, who just thinks I'm crazy, Barry understands my enthusiasm for such odd occurrences. Both he and Rod are more skilful anglers than me, but Barry also has a philosophical approach to angling similar to a Zen archer. The Zen archer aims his arrow at the target but doesn't let fly until his concentration is so intense that the target has become an extension of himself. Therefore he never misses. Similarly, there were times when Barry was so mesmerised by an approaching carp that, in his own words, *he became the carp.* And whenever that happened he never failed to catch it.

There are times when I have this same kind of unshakable conviction that I'm going to catch a particular fish, though in my case I don't even have to be near the water. I just suddenly have this preposterous realisation that, if I go to a certain spot at a certain pool at a certain time, I will catch a big fish. This intuitive confidence, this recognition of a ripe moment, doesn't occur very often, but it has never failed me and, moreover, has been instrumental in the capture of all my largest carp. However, it has also caused me the most unbearable frustration.

One late July day, just before I was due to go again to Redmire, I had this sense that I was going to encounter an outstanding fish. The weather had been hot and dry almost all month but I felt sure that, towards the end of the week, there would be a violent storm, and that would be the moment to cast. Unfortunately my old van had just suffered a terminal breakdown, but I didn't mind as I could go instead on my motorcycle. I packed my gear and was just heading up the lane from my cottage when there was a flash from inside the headlight followed by a cloud of smoke. The bike stopped. Somehow, it had blown all its fuses and burnt out the entire electrical system.

Next day I borrowed a friend's bike and was

halfway to the pool when the engine seized. I couldn't arrange any other transport in time and, that evening, the weather turned. No one had fished Redmire for a fortnight and I'm certain the big carp went rampant on the shallows. The rain was tropical and the aftermath humid and steamy. As I gazed out of my window at the dripping woods the sense of imminent monsters grew stronger, and the sense of an historic opportunity magnificently missed finally drove me to eat the furniture.

The question of the sixth sense has always seemed to me to be entirely reasonable and I have absolutely no doubt that our intuitive natures provide the key to a richer life. But too many born-again astrologers and gullible mystics have made the more uncanny aspects of the world seem spurious. In 1987 there was a lot of fuss in the papers about the new age of Aquarius, and much talk about mass hysteria, visions and curious behaviour (mostly among west-coast Americans). 'Harmonic Convergence' they called it.

'Hey!' I said to Bob. 'It sounds as if we should go down to the Avon and have a harmonic convergence with a monster barbel.'

We went down to Ringwood and first I caught an eel and then Bob, fishing a different swim, also caught an eel. Then I caught a barbel of seven pounds ten ounces and as I was releasing it Bob also caught a barbel of exactly the same weight It was the beginning of a very curious symmetry.

Later that year we visited a fishery where the barbel were quite hard to find, let alone catch, and where I'd never before caught more than one or two fish in a season. During the morning Bob had a tremendous catch, six big barbel and a brace of chub. He had to pack up at lunchtime, when I arrived, and during the afternoon I too caught six big barbel and a brace of chub. We went to Redmire in 1989 and both caught a brace of twenty pounders. They were all, I hasten to add, different fish, and all but one was twenty four pounds. Bob had never even seen Redmire, and on my last visit, eight years previously, I hadn't even had a bite.

Although Bob is a much more skilful angler than I and though, especially when we're fishing for roach or chub, he will usually catch the most, it is strange how our fishing often seems synchronised. Because we've been making an epic fishing film with the celebrated wildlife cameraman, Hugh Miles, we don't actually fish together much when we're not working, yet we still can't quite derail the wheel of fortune that rolls along with us. Last season, for instance, I only caught one twenty pounder. On that same day, at a lake a hundred miles away, Bob caught *his* only twenty pounder of the season. We tried terribly hard to break this pattern on other days and at other waters, and though we caught many more carp, we didn't manage another twenty pounder. I have just heard, as I have been reading these page proofs that Bob has landed his first monster carp. It weighed 43lbs 13 oz. In 1972 I caught *my* first monster. It too weighed 43lbs 13oz!

My strangest experience of 'coincidence' concerns not a fish but a fishing story. I often write during train journeys, especially if I'm travelling up to London, and on the day in question I boarded a train at Salisbury, found my seat and took out pen and paper. I'd been commissioned to write a piece about the sixth sense for an angling anthology edited by Tim Paisley. I wrote the title of my chapter at the top of the page: *Dowsing with a Fishing Rod*. The man sitting opposite me suddenly commented on my Hardy fishing bag (I use it for carrying manuscripts and photographs when I'm visiting publishers).

'That's just the kind of bag I've been looking for,' he said.

So I stopped writing and we discussed bags for a moment. Then, as my fellow traveller had learnt that I was an angler, he told me in return that he was a professional dowser. His name was Hans Obersdorf. I'd never met a real dowser before, but he didn't just dowse for water, his speciality was dowsing for wild animals.

'Here,' I said, 'You've seen this bag. Now let me show you the title of this chapter.'

CHAPTER TWENTY THREE

The Writing on the Water

I am now back where I began, sitting at the corner of the lake under the great oak, with only just enough light in the sky to see what I'm scribbling. The trees opposite are now simply symbols of trees, so black against the afterglow they have only two dimensions. Several carp are moving just below the surface in the middle distance making luminous ripples. The swallows have returned to their nests and the swifts have risen to their roosts in the sky. All the songbirds have fallen silent and now there is just a tawny owl calling in the woods and the fluttering of the bats.

This is the hour of the Mollies. According to a couple of local lads I spoke to last week, one of the grottos round the lake is haunted by the Mollies.

'What are the Mollies?' I asked.

'No one knows for sure,' they said. 'But they come out at night, when no-one's around. Only when it's special do they come out in daylight.'

I told Shaun about this when he came down to

161

have his first ever glimpse of the lake, three days ago (he wants to join the syndicate now). We stood talking in a gap in the trees, looking out across sunlit water. There was no evidence of fish, but just as we were turning to go we saw an apparition. It was as if someone had appeared out of thin air next to us. A big pale carp was hanging in midwater about two yards from our feet. There had been nothing there when we'd arrived, the water was less than a yard deep and (on that day) crystal clear. The fish was looking directly at us so that we couldn't move for fear of disturbing it.

Then Shaun said, 'That's not a carp, that's a Molly!'

It seemed a perfectly obvious explanation in the circumstances. For nearly five minutes we watched it and it watched us, then it turned and very slowly and lethargically glided away into the depths. If Mollies could transform themselves into fish, we reasoned that it was probably futile to fish the lake as maybe *all* the big carp were Mollies. And even if you did somehow manage to hook one you would be sure to lose it. Maybe they were more widespread than we realised, haunting lakes and ponds across the country. This would explain why so many fish escaped; every carp hooked and lost was a Molly.

But Mollies or no Mollies, it is time I was getting back. It must be nearly half past ten and I seem to have been here for an age. Though it would be pleasant to curl up in a sleeping bag and dream of Mollies till dawn, I prefer the thought of the smile that awaits me when I reach my cottage. The small folk will be asleep and I can sit in my chair with a glass of port and tell the Gaffer about my memorable day. And of course this lake will ripple home with me and overflow into my sleep.

I've reeled in for the last time, but already I'm thinking about my next visit, wondering where I'm going to fish and what I might discover. Will there be more chances? Will the big fish come within casting range again? Wll this place continue to seem so perfect or, as has happened at other places, will its marvellous qualities become dulled by familiarity?

The blue light lingers quite brightly in the north-west, but the lake shimmers darkly. The carp are still moving slowly across the surface, far off now, trailing pale lines, circles and curves, like writing on the water.

163

The following books are also published by:

Merlin Unwin Books
21 Corve Street, Ludlow
Shropshire SY8 1DA

The One That Got Away

or tales of days when fish triumphed over anglers
With original woodcuts by Christopher Wormell

'The one that got away' is the best-known phrase in fishing. Every angler has at least one story of being outwitted by a huge fish. A refrain of the angler, a taunt from those who live with them; it neatly sums up the way in which anglers are obsessed with the fish they almost caught. Yet to hear a fisherman tell the story of an escapee leviathan is to gain a great insight into why he fishes in the first place and why his sport is the most popular in the world.

This is a collection of original stories from well-known angling enthusiasts and writers. They tell of unforgettable fish hooked and lost, of glimpsed monsters which haunt the imagination and draw the narrator back to a particular lake or river, time and again, in search of a re-match.

David Steel loses his first-ever salmon after an epic struggle on the Ettrick, George Melly is upstaged by a giant Usk brown trout, Jeremy Paxman describes a hilarious adventure in Sri Lanka, Max Hastings battles it out on the Naver, Bernard Venables - extending the definition of 'fish' - describes a thrilling but tragic whaling adventure in the Azores. Chris Yates, holder of the British carp record, tells of his close encounter with an even bigger carp, David Profumo is humiliated by a 400lb shark, Brian Clarke has his angling life marked by a monster pike and Conrad Voss Bark actually helped his fish get away - and he swears it came back to say 'thank you'.

The pens of sixteen of the finest fishing writers have been at work and the result makes compelling reading for anglers of every persuasion.

Price: £16.95 ISBN: 1-873674-02-3

An Angler for all Seasons
the best of H. T. Sheringham

H. T. Sheringham ranks among the finest fishing writers of the twentieth century. Here is a collection of the very best of his angling experiences, taken mainly from his six fishing books and from *The Field*, for which he was angling editor.

No fish escaped his interest, even if it did sometimes escape his creel - carp, tench, chub, pike, roach, salmon and trout - all were pursued with equal gusto.

He takes the reader on a journey without frontiers, from the reservoirs (Blagdon in its opening years) to the finest chalk-streams in England, from overgrown canals to Welsh salmon rivers. No snob, he knew only the joy of the sport.

He is funny, he is moving and - most rare - he is modest about his all-round skills with rod and line. If you are new to Sheringham, *An Angler for all Seasons* will convert you into one of his many admirers.

In 1903, while fishing on the Lambourn, Sheringham met William Senior, the Editor of *The Field*, and was offered the job of Angling Editor of that magazine. It was a job he held until his death in 1930, at the age of 54.

Besides his regular magazine articles, he wrote several novels and six fishing books, including *An Angler's Hours*, *An Open Creel*, *Elements of Angling*, *Coarse Fishing*, *Trout Fishing: Memories and Morals* and *Fishing: its Cause, Treatment and Cure*.

He wrote with passion about the pleasures of coarse fishing which, unusually for his generation, he rated as highly as trout and salmon fishing.

The essays in this anthology have been chosen and introduced by Tom Fort, the angling correspondent of the *Financial Times*.

Price £16.95 ISBN: 1 873674 04 X

167

The Best of Bernard Venables

the illustrated memoir of an angler

Bernard Venables

Bernard Venables is a remarkable angler by the standards of any generation. In his time he has caught record fish, he was a co-founder and director of *Angling Times*, probably the most successful fishing journal of modern times, he founded the popular but short-lived magazine *Creel*, he invented the cartoon character Mr Crabtree (the inspiration of so many budding anglers), he regularly broadcast on television (*Angler's Corner*) and radio and, last but by no means least, he is a distinguished artist whose paintings (many of which have been of fish, rivers, anglers and lakes) are much sought-after by collectors.

He has known and fished with the likes of Richard Walker, Charles Ritz, Frank Sawyer, Oliver Kite, Terry Thomas, Lionel Sweet - indeed many of the most famous fishing personalities of the past 60 years. His clear recollection of conversations and adventures in their company are wonderful to read.

This beautifully illustrated book - part angler's auto-biography, part artist's retrospective - will delight all Venables fans. It is the testimony, in pictures and words, of one of the great angling characters of the twentieth century.

Price: £19.95   ISBN: 1 873674 06 6

Publication: April 1993